Utilize este código QR para se cadastrar de forma mais rápida:

Ou, se preferir, entre em:

www.richmond.com.br/ac/livroportal

e siga as instruções para ter acesso aos conteúdos exclusivos do **Portal e Livro Digital**

CÓDIGO DE ACESSO:
A 00146 JBEANS 2 99490

Faça apenas um cadastro. Ele será válido para:

 MODERNA   **Richmond**   SANTILLANA ESPAÑOL

6624070755 JELLY BEANS 2 LA_213

CB053074

De los árboles a los libros, sostenibilidad en todo el camino

Da semente ao livro,
sustentabilidade por todo o caminho

Plantar bosques

La madera usada como materia prima para nuestro papel viene de plantaciones renovables, o sea, no es fruto de deforestación. Este tipo de plantación genera millares de empleos para los agricultores y ayuda a recuperar las áreas ambientales degradadas.

Plantar florestas

A madeira que serve de matéria-prima para nosso papel vem de plantio renovável, ou seja, não é fruto de desmatamento. Essa prática gera milhares de empregos para agricultores e ajuda a recuperar áreas ambientais degradadas.

Fabricar papel e imprimir libros

Toda la cadena de producción de papel, desde la fabricación de la celulosa hasta la encuadernación del libro, tiene los correspondientes certificados y cumple los patrones internacionales de procesamiento sostenible y las buenas prácticas ambientales.

Fabricar papel e imprimir livros

Toda a cadeia produtiva do papel, desde a produção de celulose até a encadernação do livro, é certificada, cumprindo padrões internacionais de processamento sustentável e boas práticas ambientais.

Crear contenido

Los profesionales involucrados en la elaboración de nuestras soluciones educativas tienen como objetivo una educación para la vida basada en la curaduría editorial, la diversidad de visiones y la responsabilidad socioambiental.

Criar conteúdo

Os profissionais envolvidos na elaboração de nossas soluções educacionais buscam uma educação para a vida pautada por curadoria editorial, diversidade de olhares e responsabilidade socioambiental.

Construir proyectos de vida

Ofrecer una solución educativa Santillana Español es un acto de compromiso con el futuro de las nuevas generaciones y posibilita una alianza entre las escuelas y las familias en la misión de educar.

Construir projetos de vida

Oferecer uma solução educacional Santillana Español é um ato de comprometimento com o futuro das novas gerações, possibilitando uma relação de parceria entre escolas e famílias na missão de educar!

SANTILLANA ESPAÑOL

Apoio:
TWO SIDES
www.twosides.org.br

Para saber más, escanea el código QR.
Accede a *http://mod.lk/sostenab*

Fotografe o código QR e conheça melhor esse caminho.
Saiba mais em *http://mod.lk/sostenab*

2

Jelly beans

This is my book.

_____

Rebecca Williams & Katy Smith

Student's Book

Richmond

Sally

Teacher

Tom

 **Point and stick.**

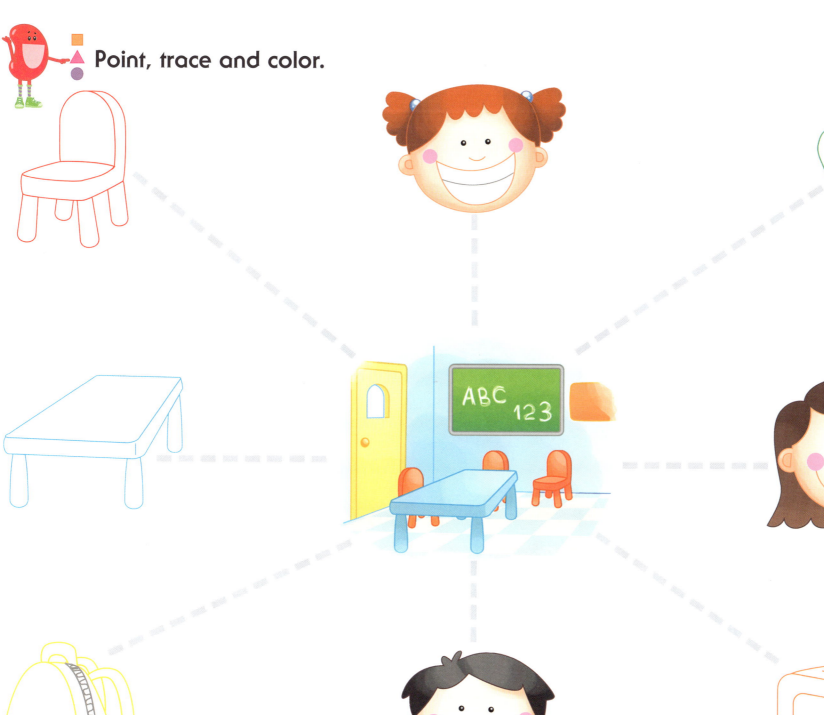

Point, trace and color.

Match, stick and trace.

Look and color.

Point and color.

Jellybeans 2

Trace, count and stick.

Look and color.

Look, color and trace.

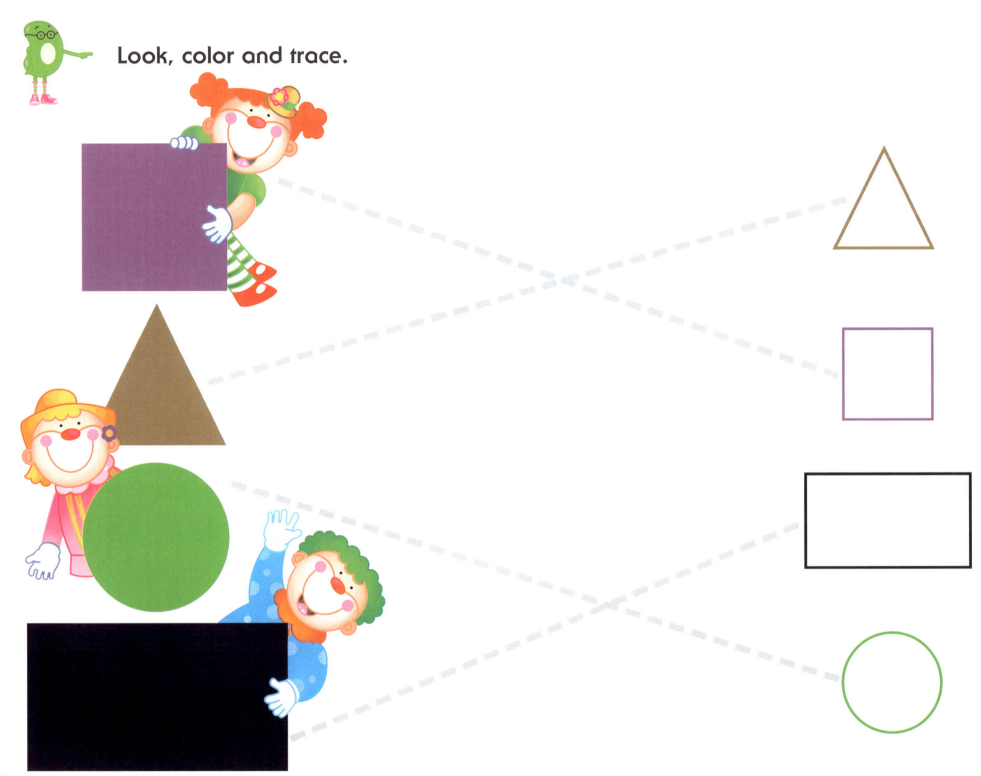

Jellybeans 2

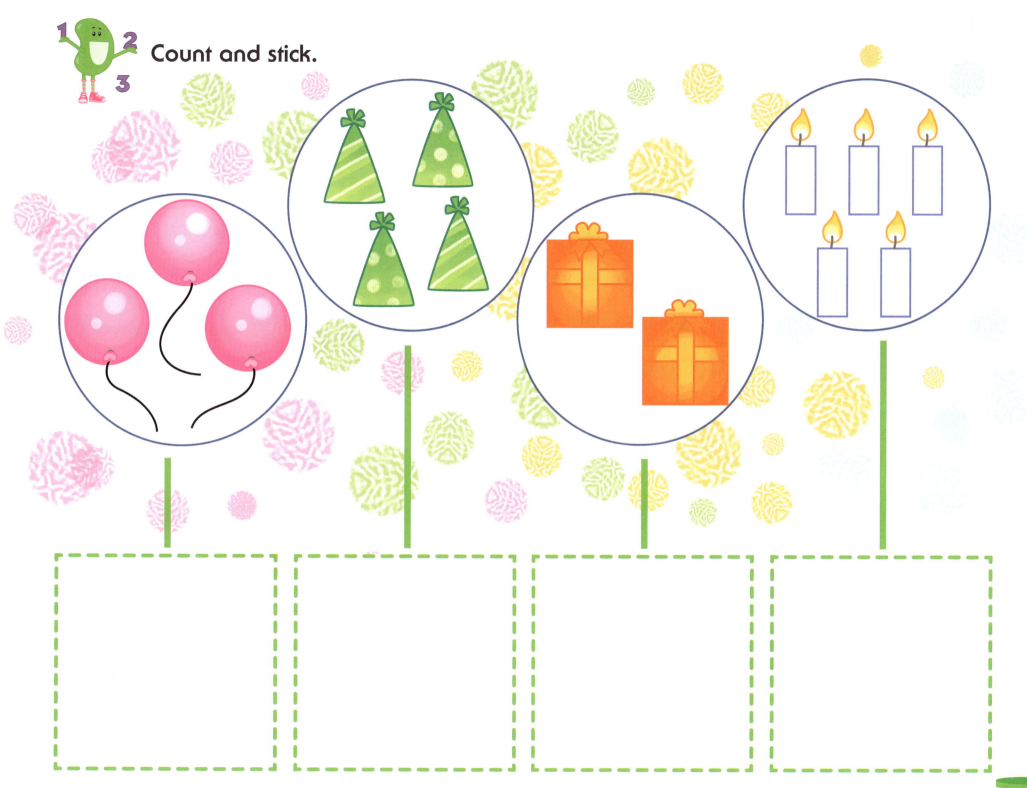

Count and stick.

Look and color.

Home and family

Unit 3

Point and stick.

Look and color.

Look and stick.

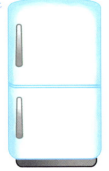

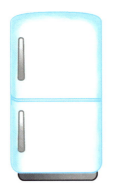

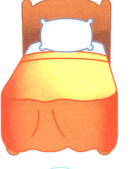

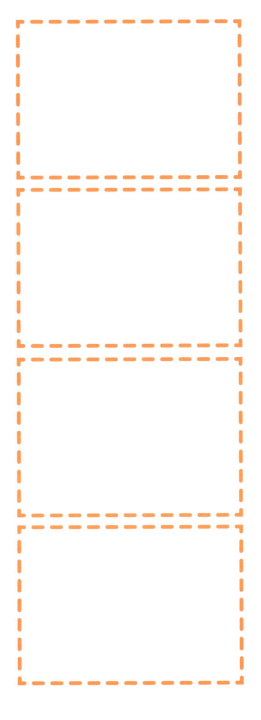

Look and circle.

Look and match.

Jellybeans 2

On the farm

Unit 4

Point and stick.

Look and circle.

Trace and count.

 Count and color.

6   7   8

Count, stick and color.

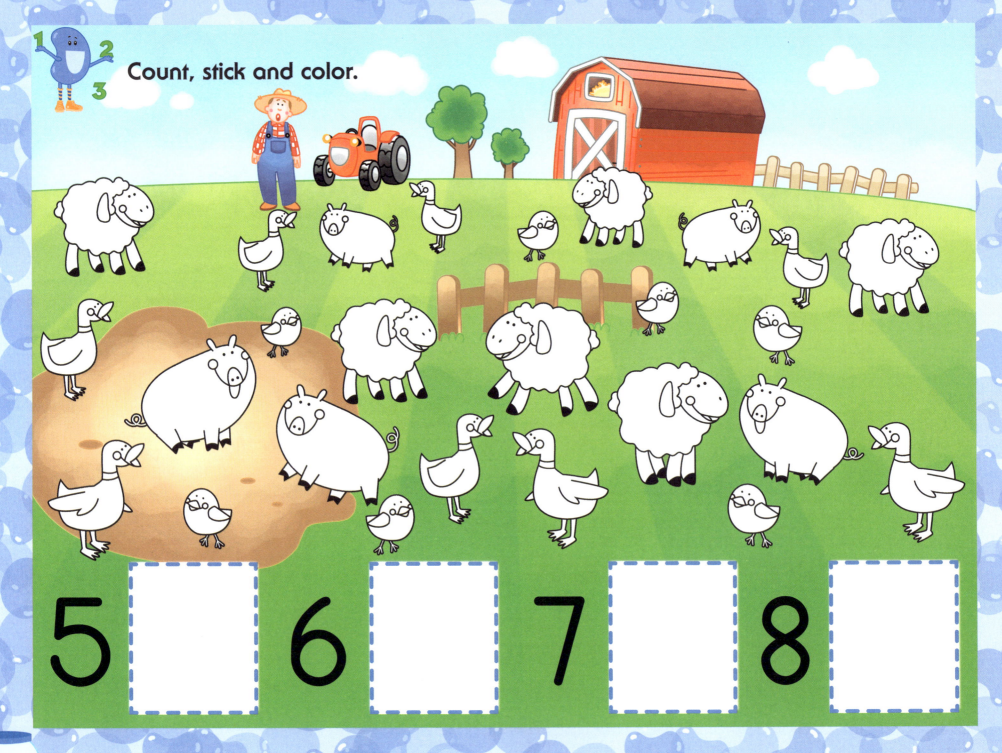

5 6 7 8

My body

Unit 5

Look and stick.

Look and trace.

Point and stick.

Look and color.

Look and circle.

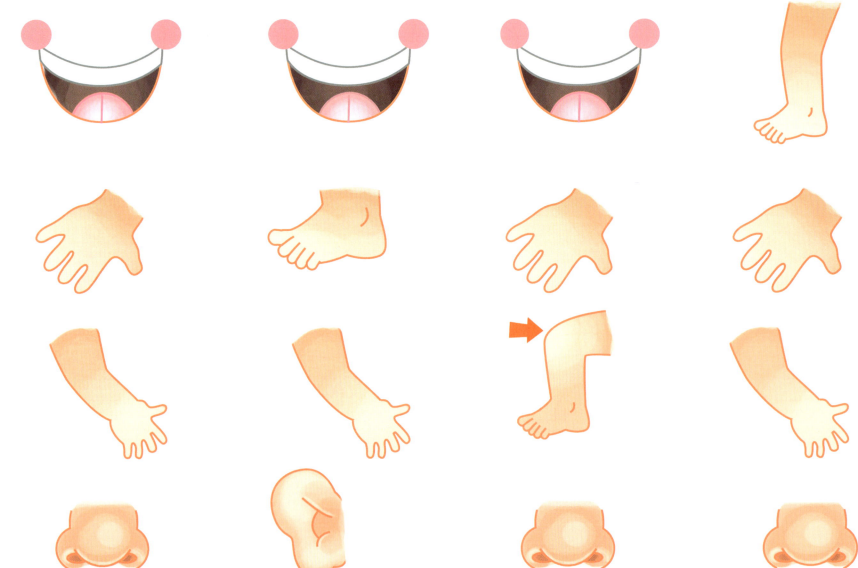

Clothes and weather

Unit 6

Look and stick.

Look and trace.

Look, stick and trace.

Look, circle and color.

Look and color.

The circus

Look, trace and stick.

Jelly beans 2

Look, match and color.

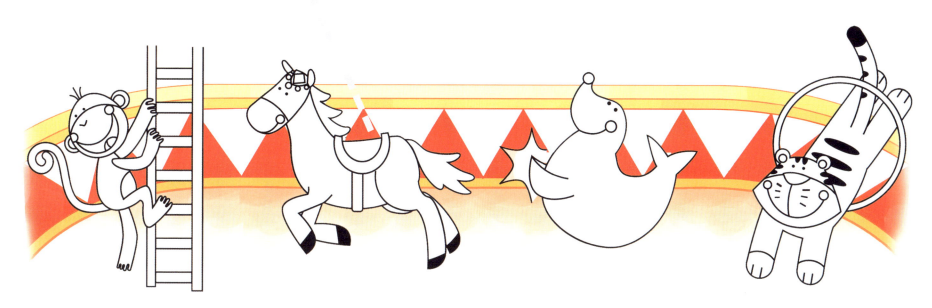

Point and stick.

Count, color and trace.

Trace and color.

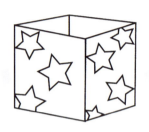

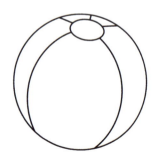

Food and drink

Unit 8

Look and stick.

Color and trace.

Look and stick.

Look, circle and color.

Look, trace and color.

Unit 1 School is fun

glue stick

pencil case

schoolbag

crayon

scissors

pencil

Unit 2 Party time

cake

candle

balloon

party hat

ice cream cone

present

sofa

bathtub

toilet

stove

fridge

dresser

sink

closet

horse

chick

cow

sheep

hen

duck

pig

goat

farmer

Jellybeans 2

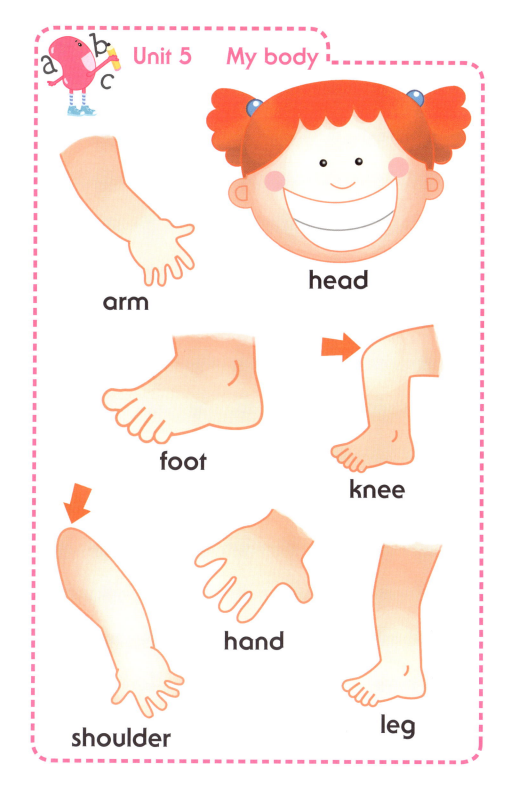

Unit 5   My body

arm

head

foot

knee

shoulder

hand

leg

Unit 6   Clothes and weather

pants

sweater

shorts

T-shirt

cap

dress

socks

shoes

skirt

Picture dictionary   53

Unit 7 The circus

acrobat

tiger

seal

elephant

monkey

clown

bear

Unit 8 Food and drink

broccoli

lemonade

French fries

peas

fish

juice

spaghetti

soup

chicken

Jellybean awards this certificate to

(NAME)

for completing

Jelly beans 2

CONGRATULATIONS!

2

Jelly beans

Rebecca Williams & Katy Smith

Activity Book

Trace, color, glue and cut.

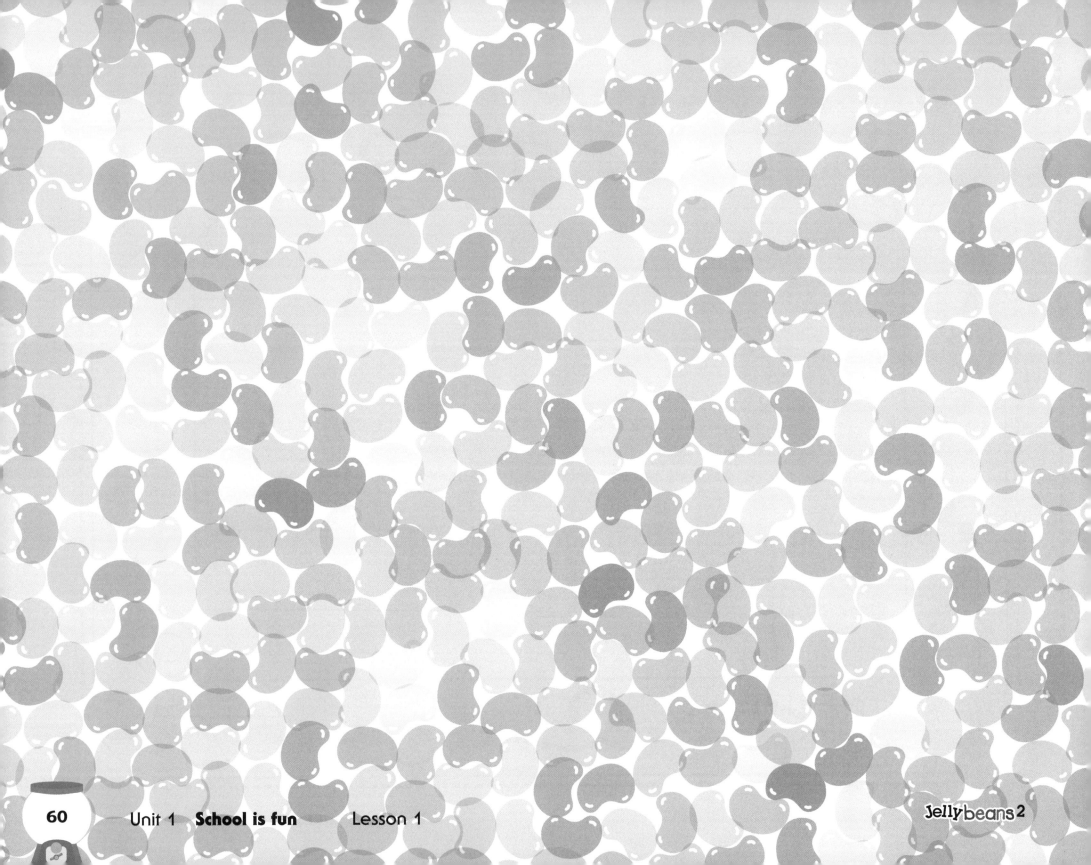

Color, cut and glue.

School

ABC
123
△□○

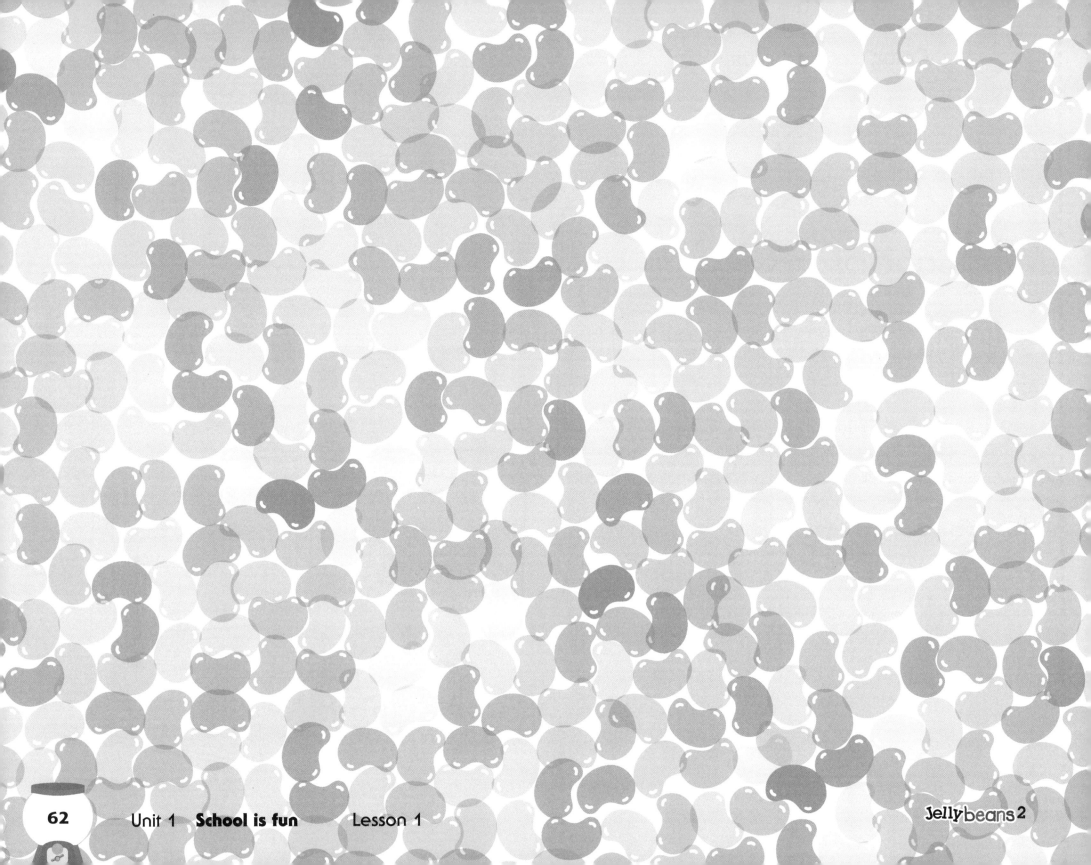

*Jelly*beans 2

Color, cut and play *Concentration.*

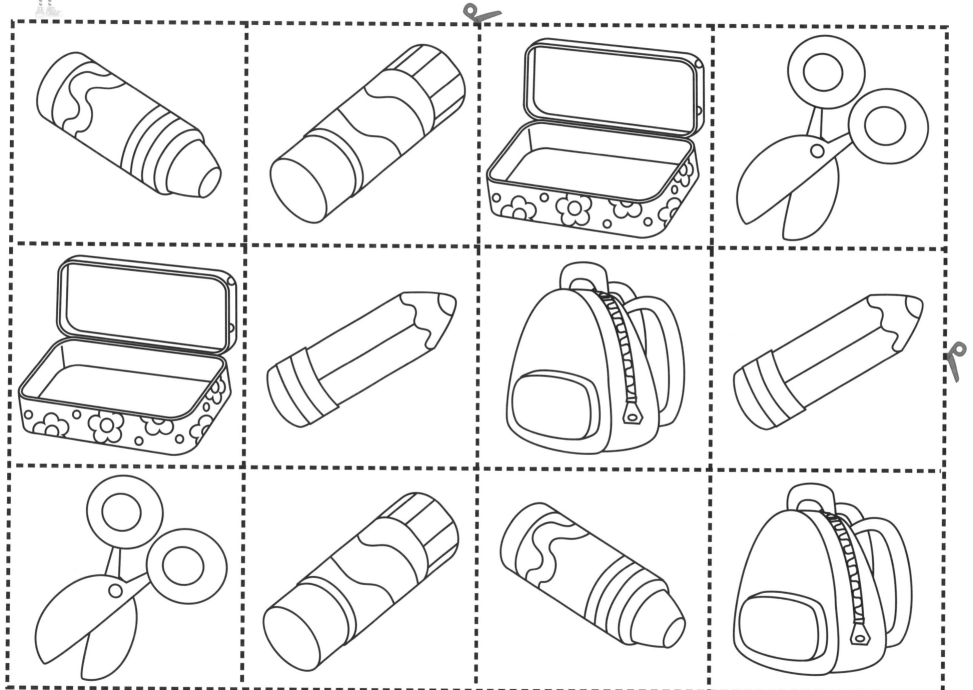

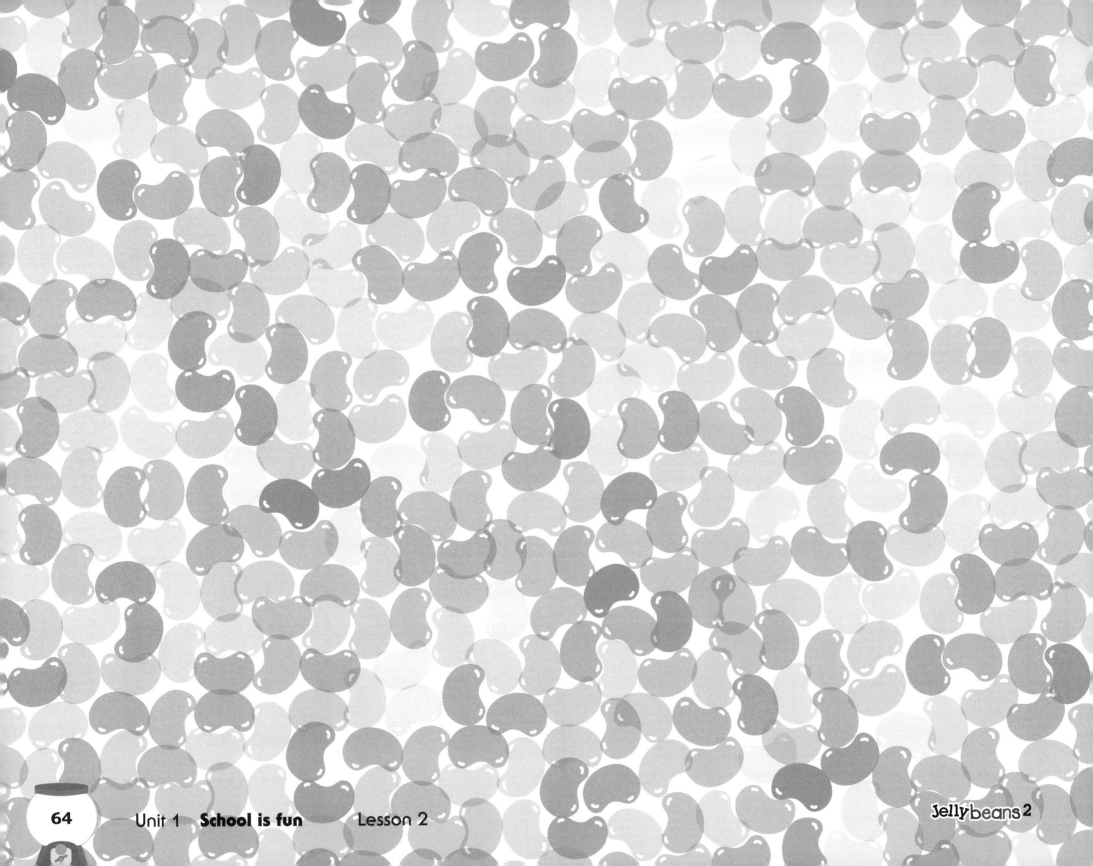

Finger-paint and cut.

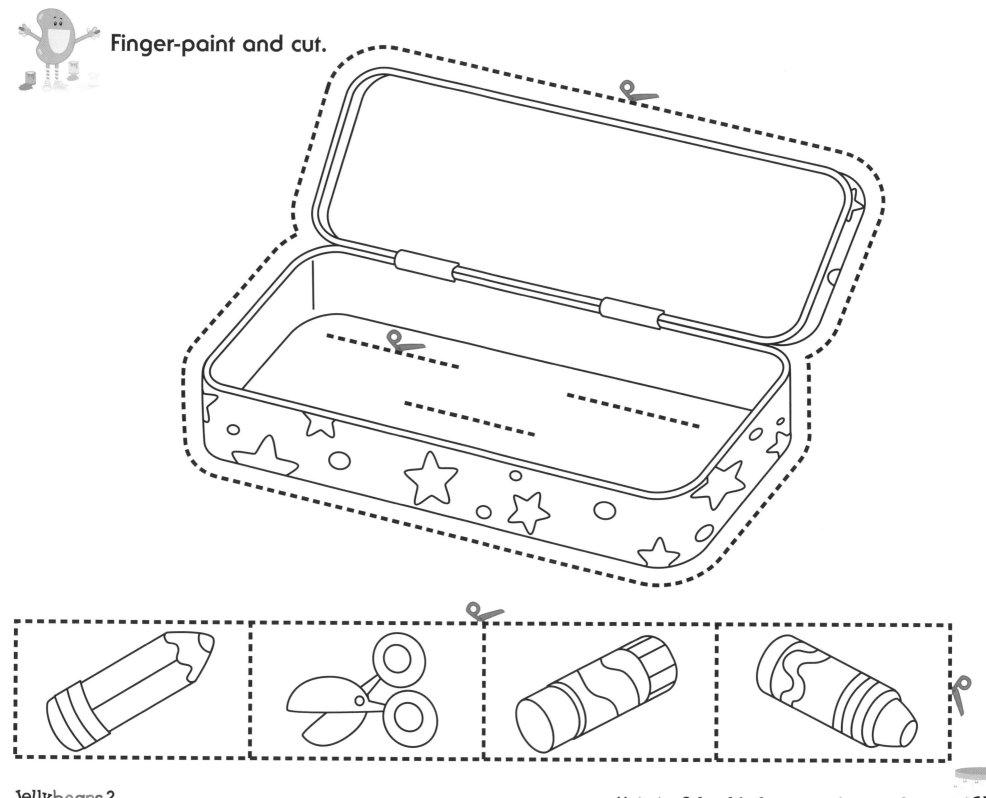

Color, cut and glue.

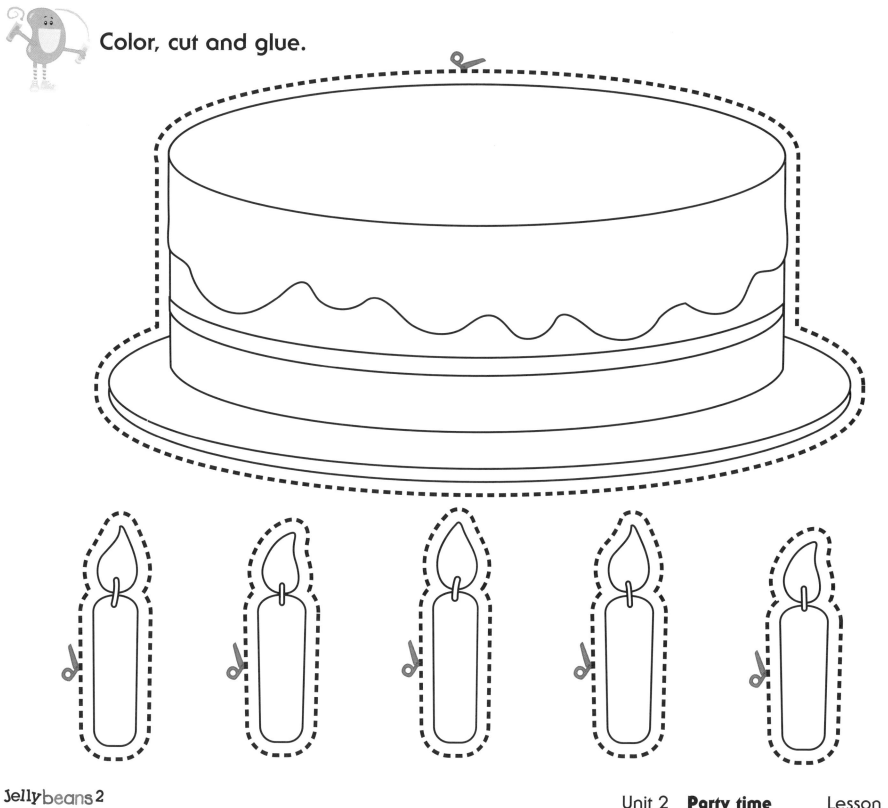

Paint, glue, cut and assemble.

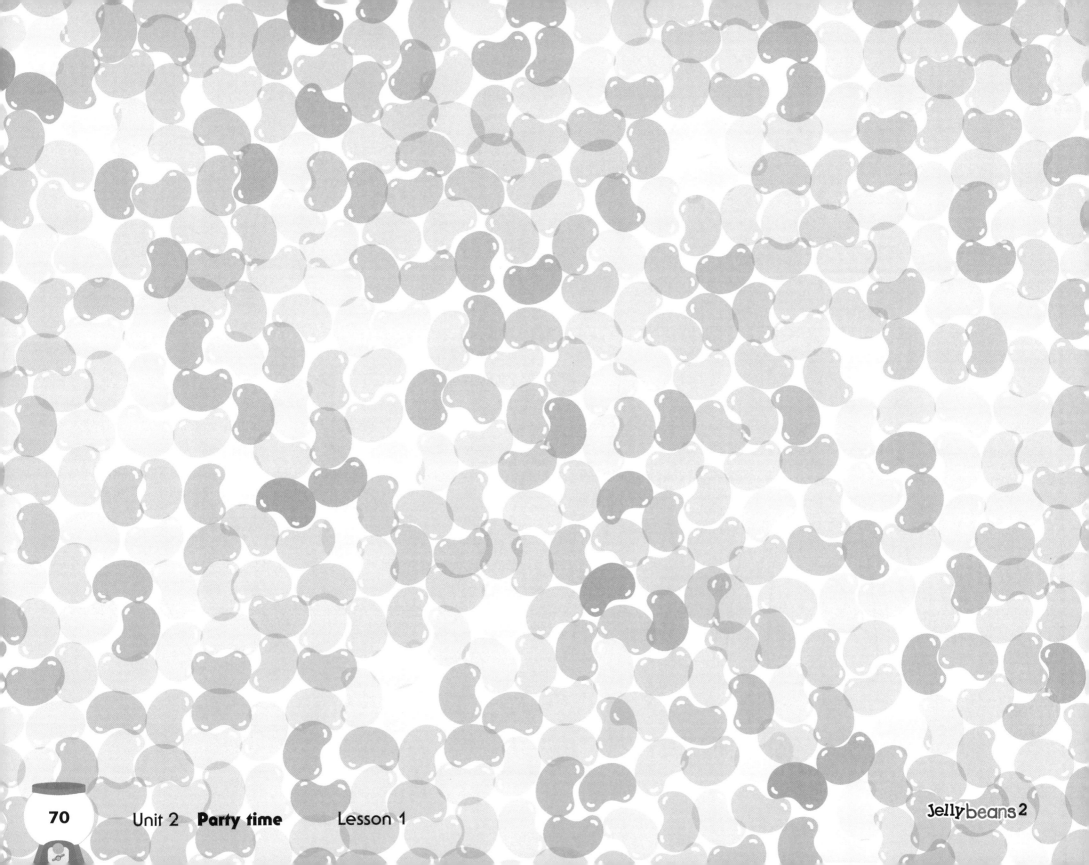

Jellybeans 2

Look, color and glue.

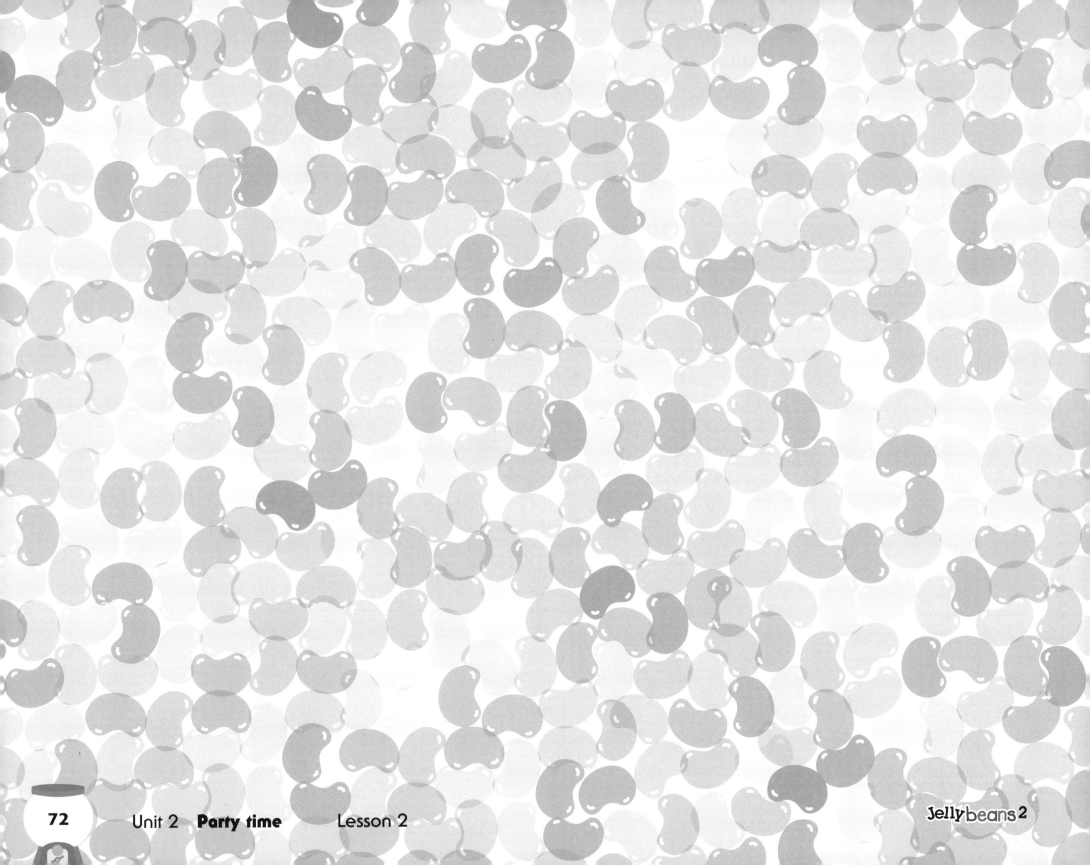

Jelly beans 2

Color, glue, cut and assemble.

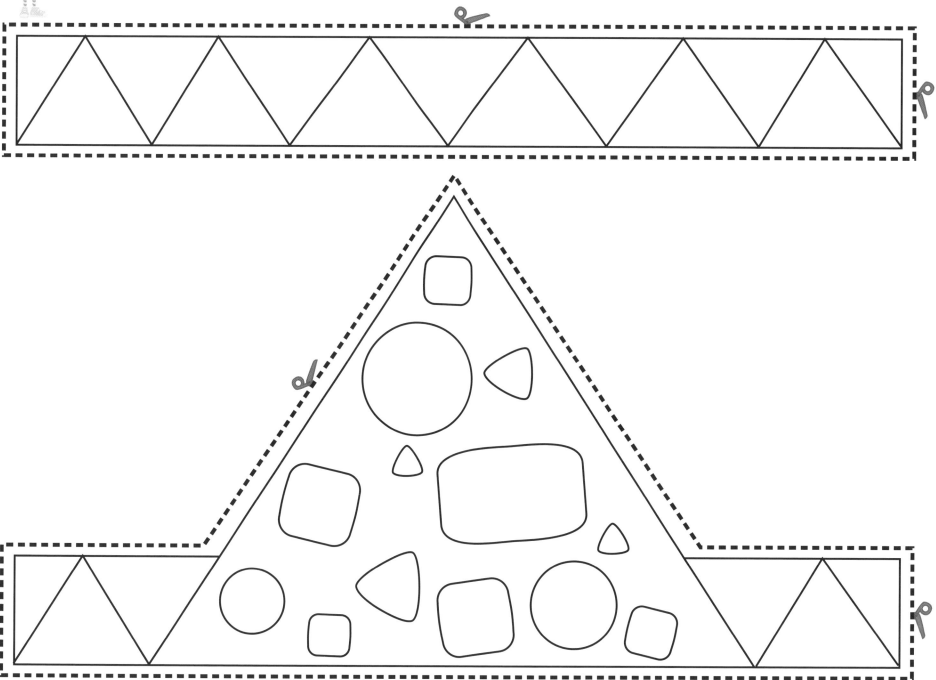

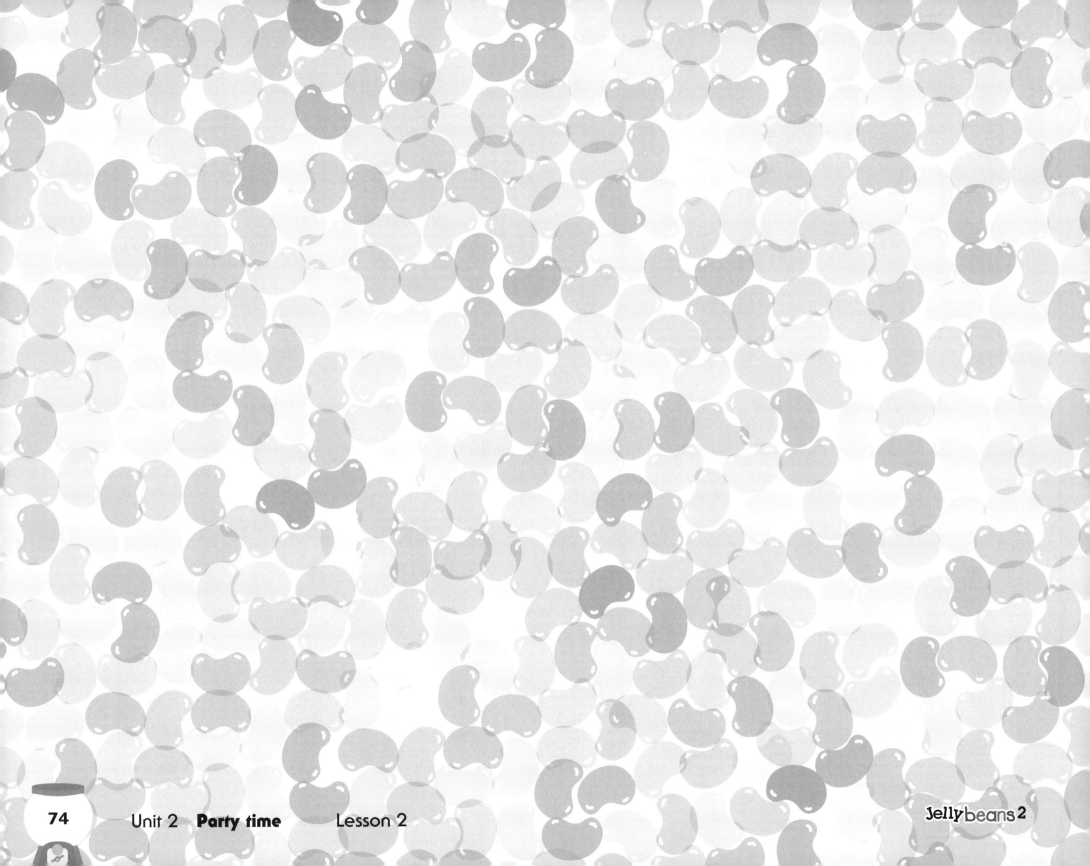

Jellybeans 2

Color, cut and assemble.

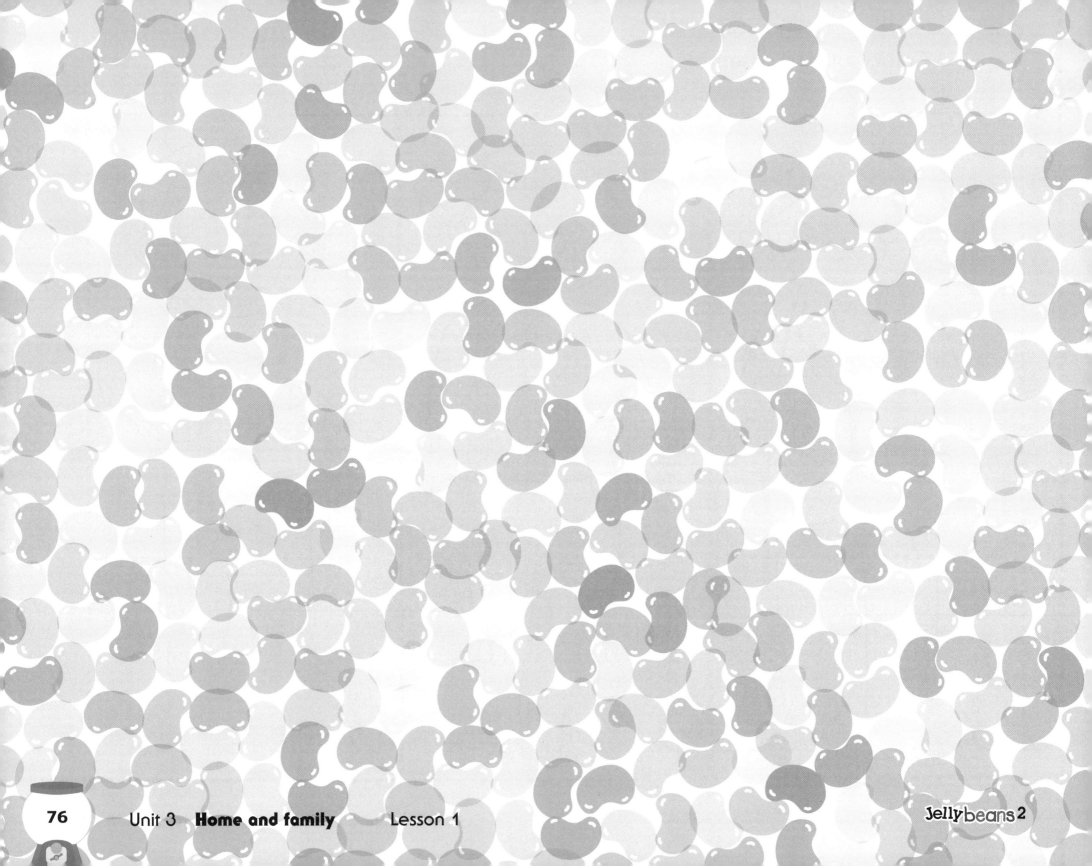

Color, cut and glue.

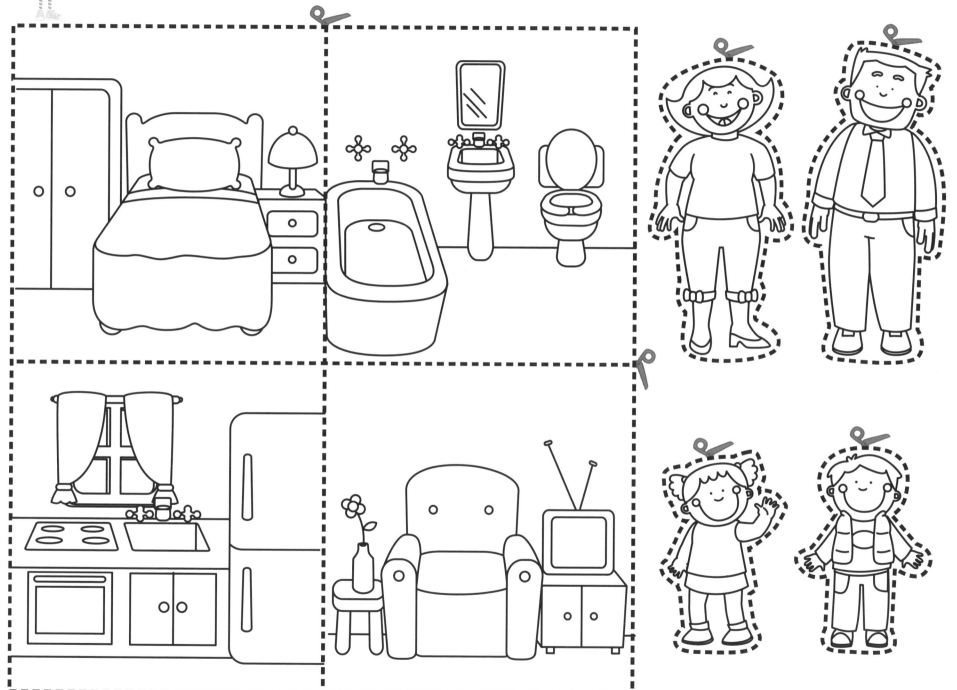

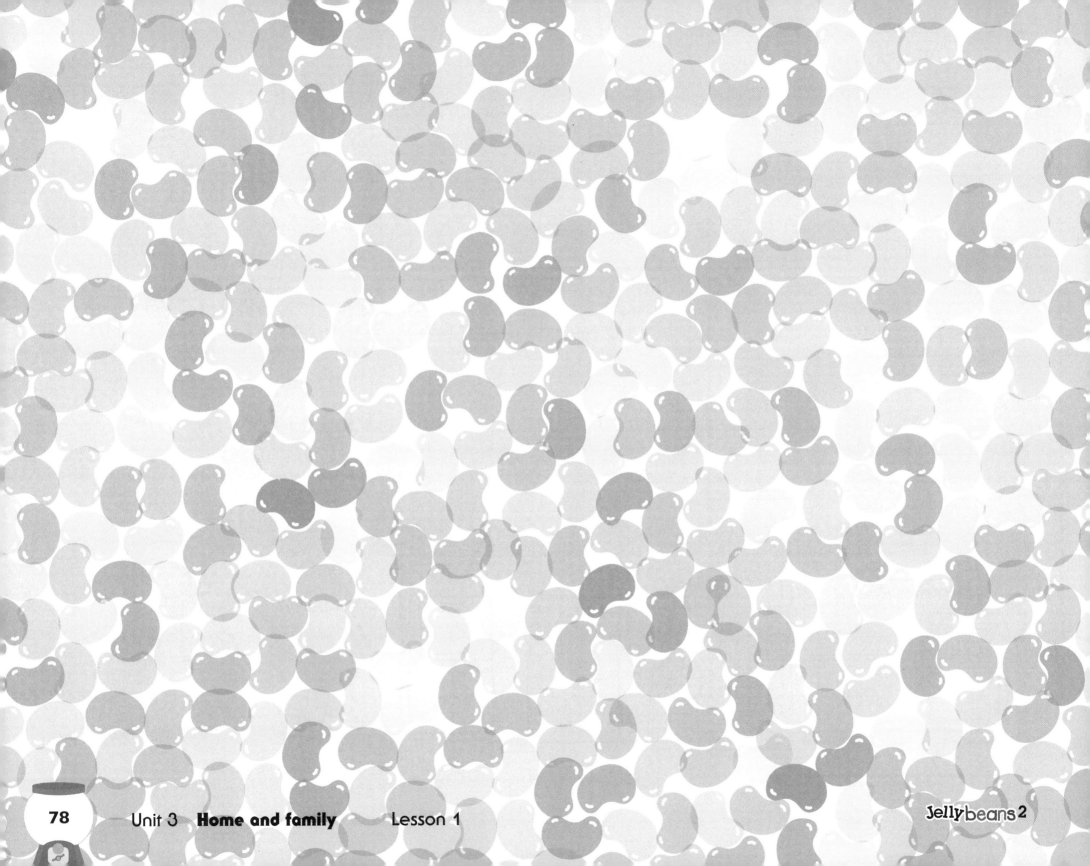

Jellybeans 2

Paint, cut and glue.

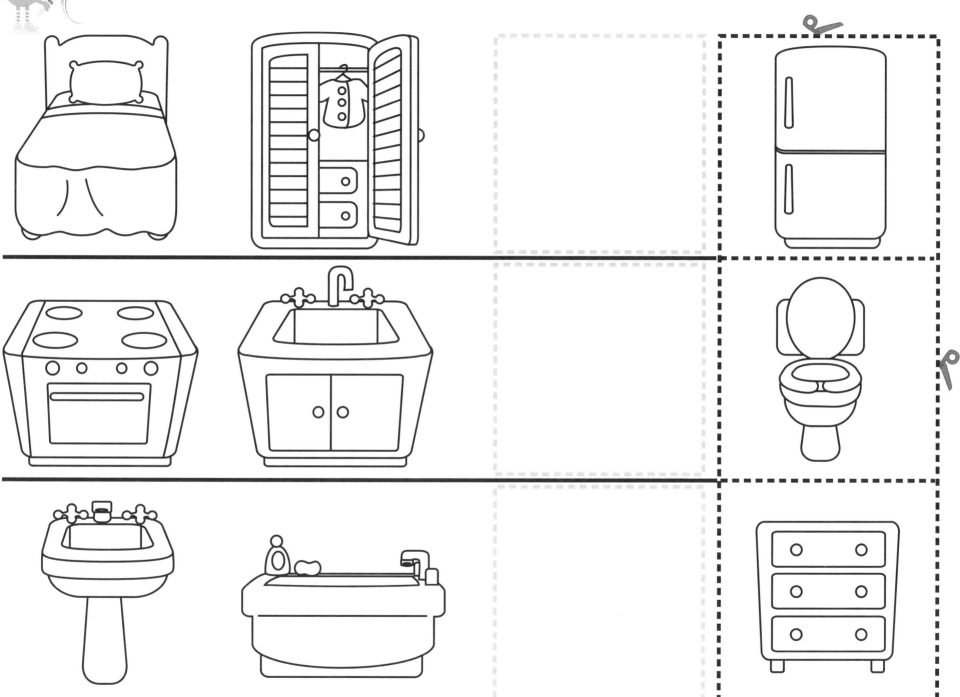

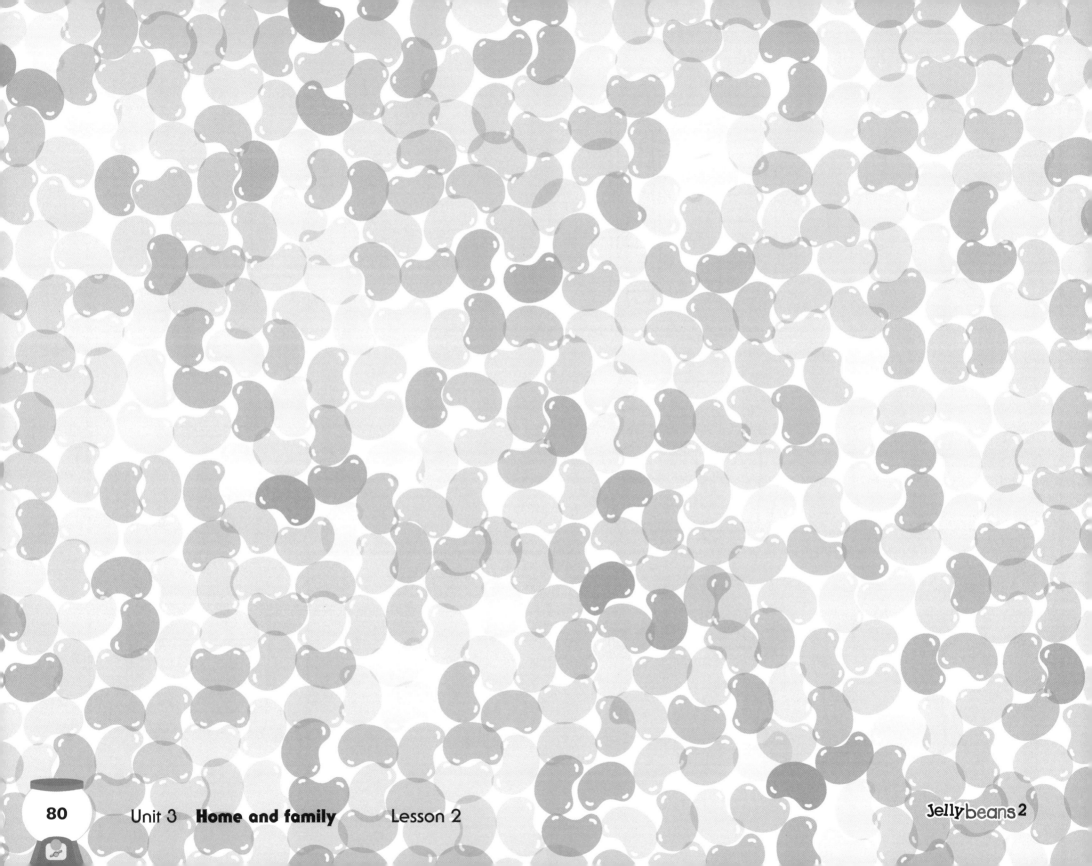

Color, cut and glue.

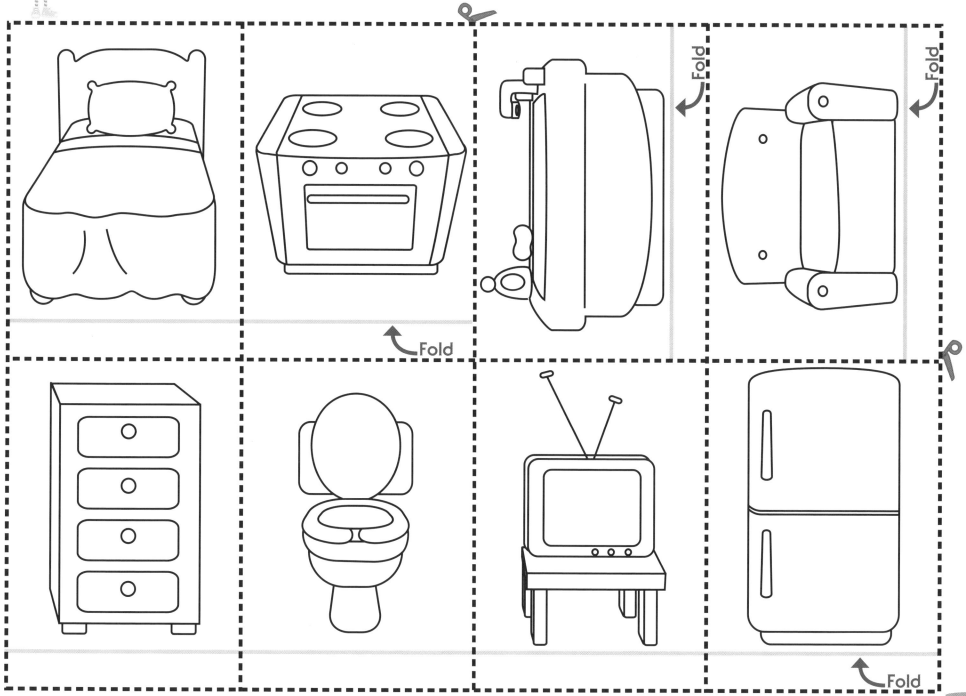

Fold

Fold

Fold

Fold

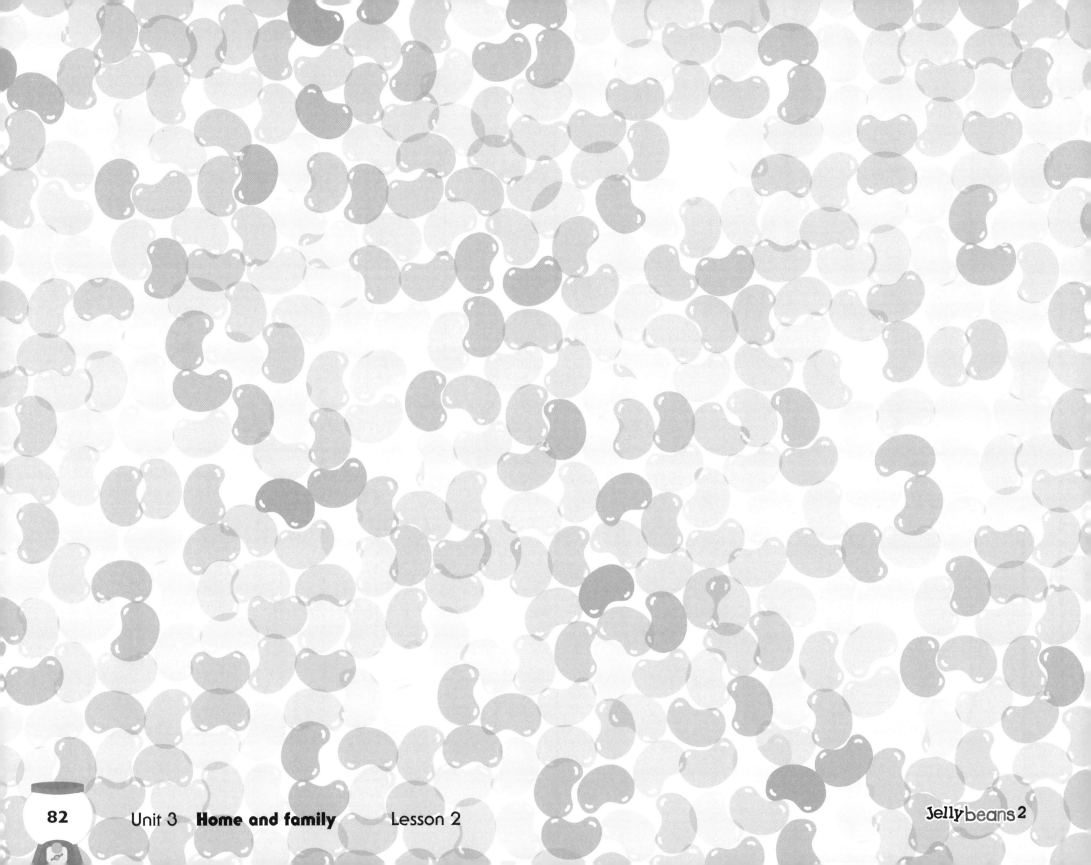

Jellybeans 2

Paint, cut and fold.

1

8

L

9

Fold 2

3

4

5

Fold

Fold

Fold

Color, cut and assemble.

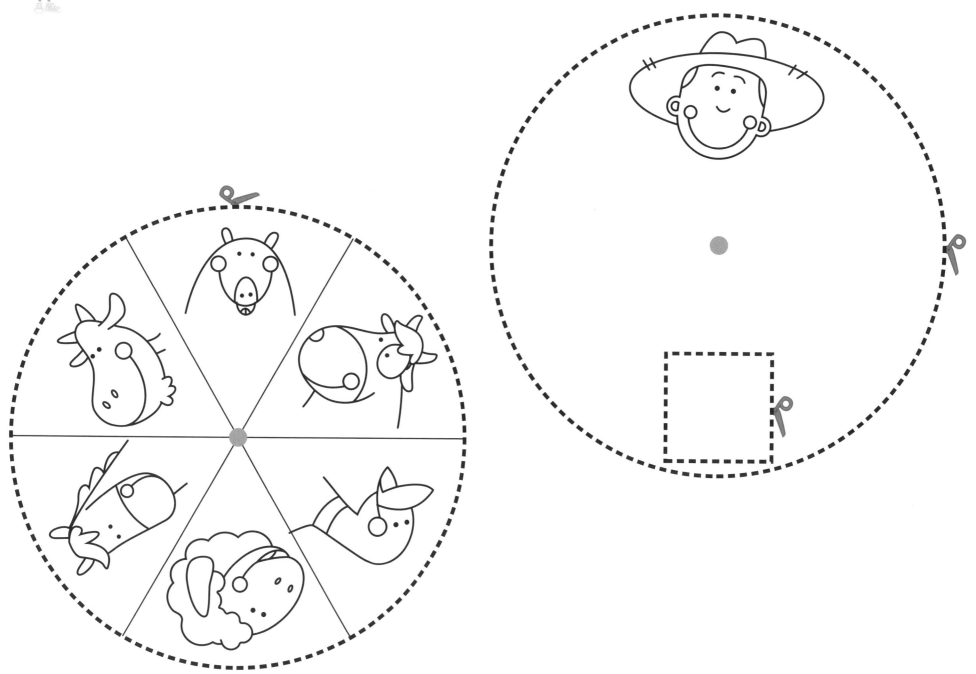

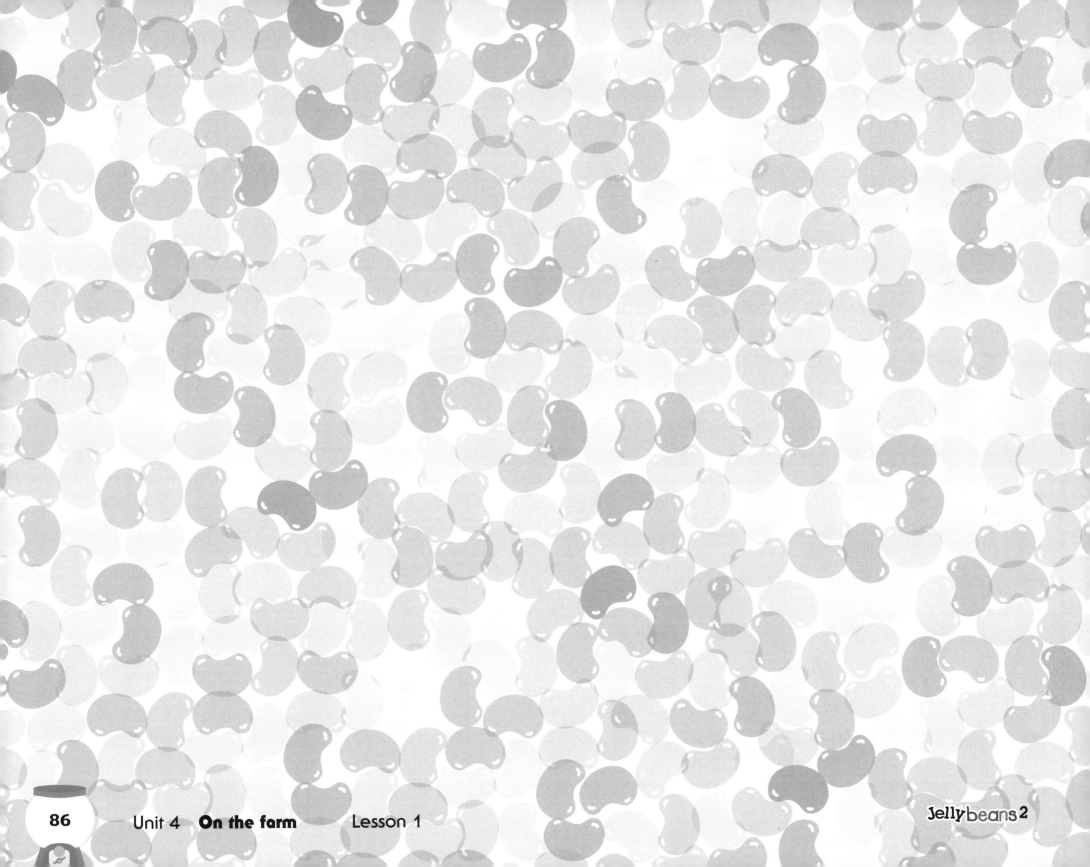

Jellybeans 2

Color, cut and assemble.

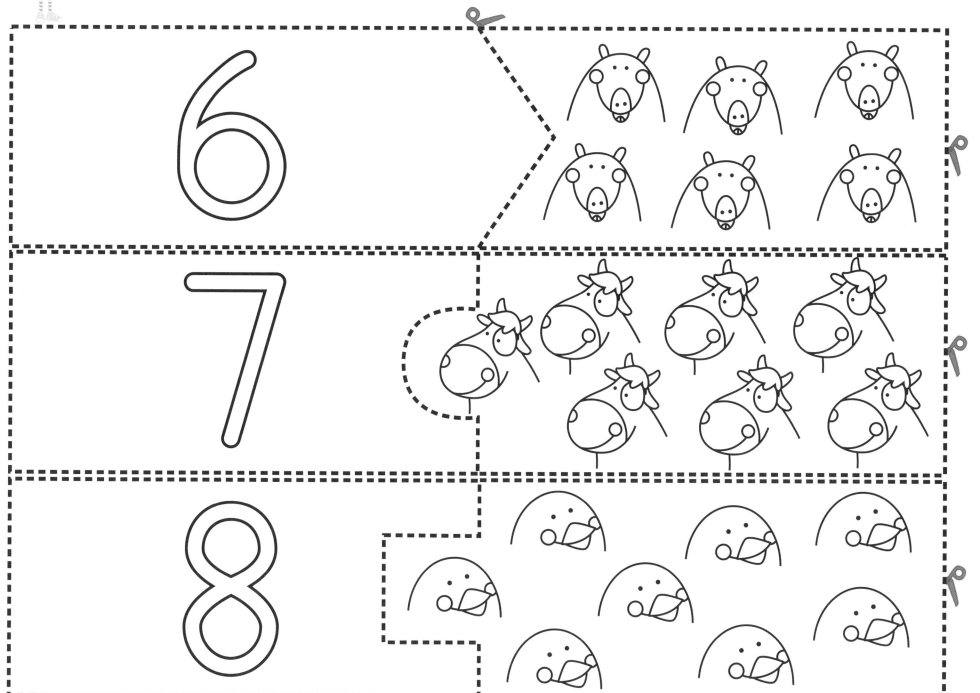

6

7

8

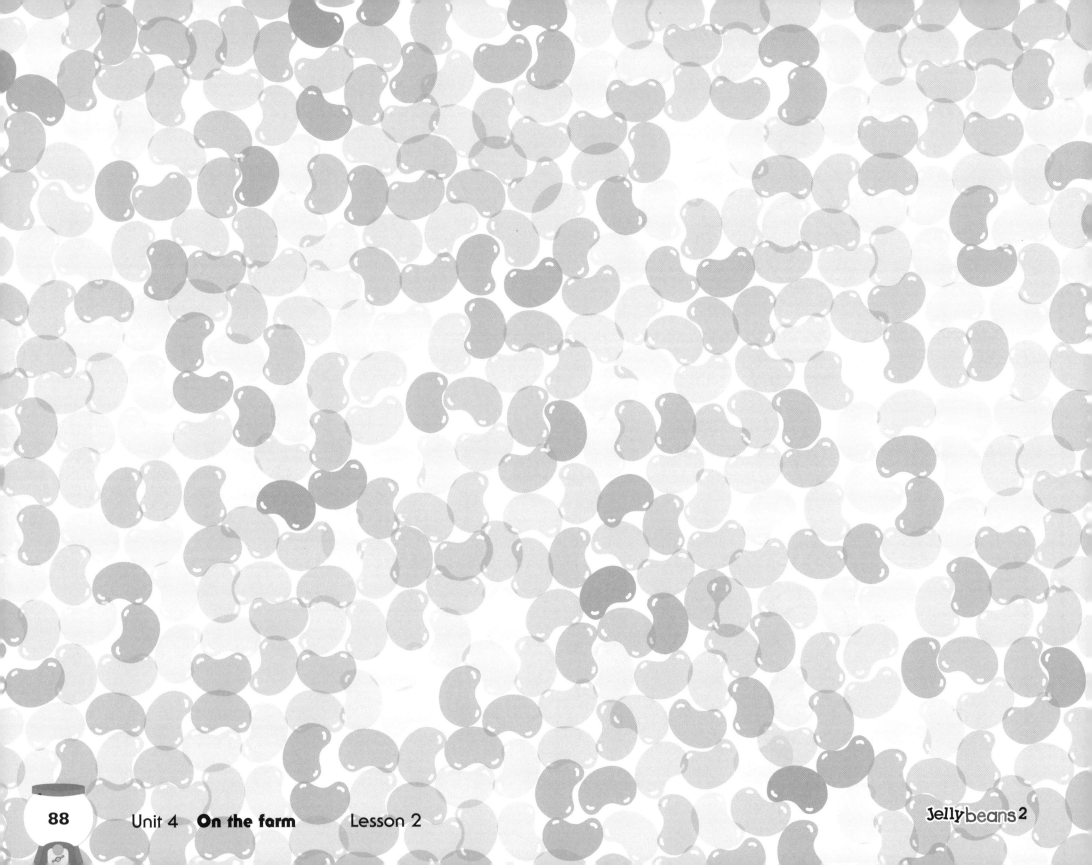

Paint, cut and assemble.

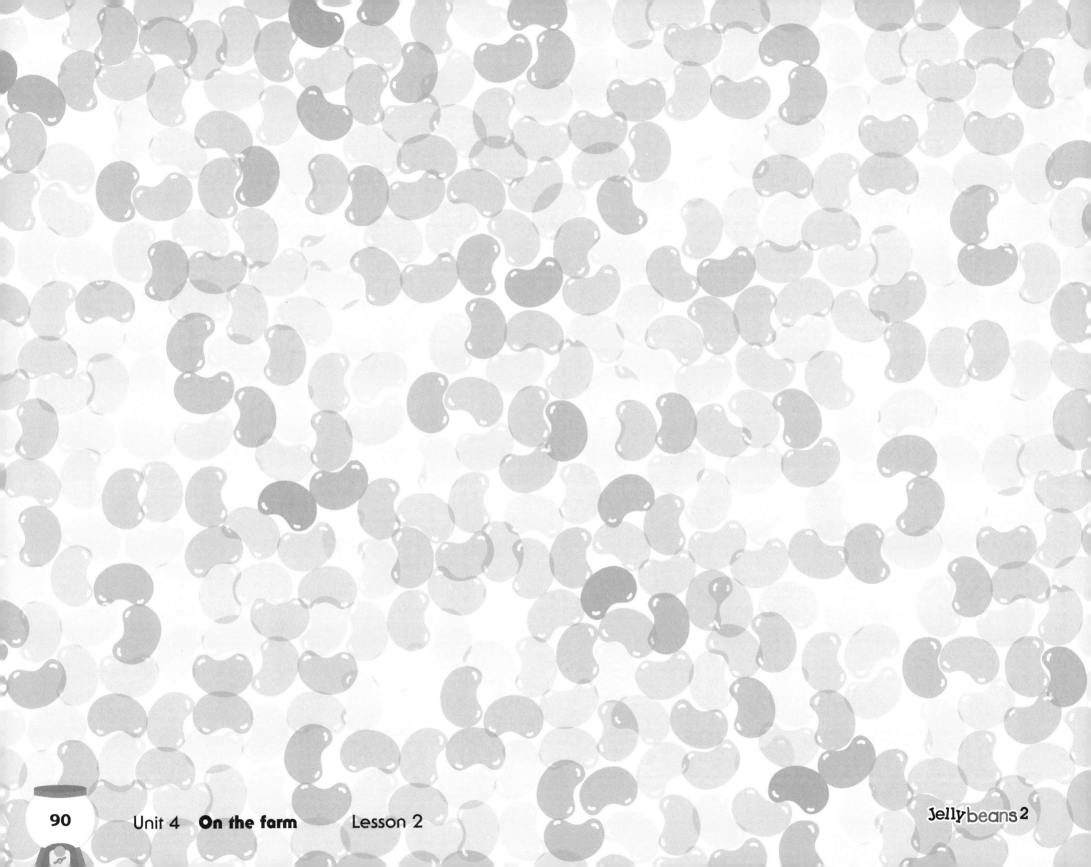

Jellybeans 2

 **Color, glue, cut and assemble.**

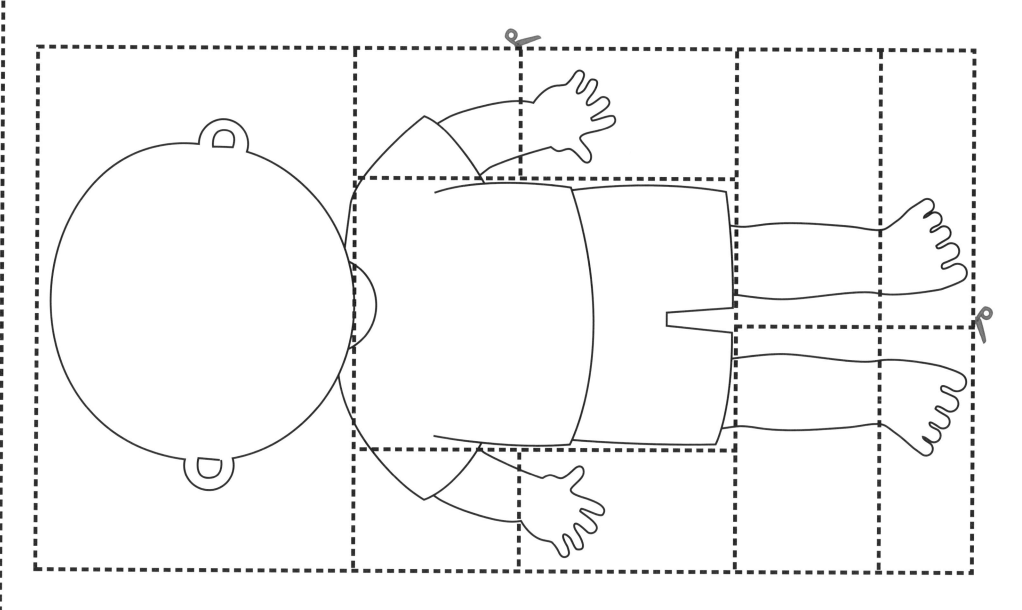

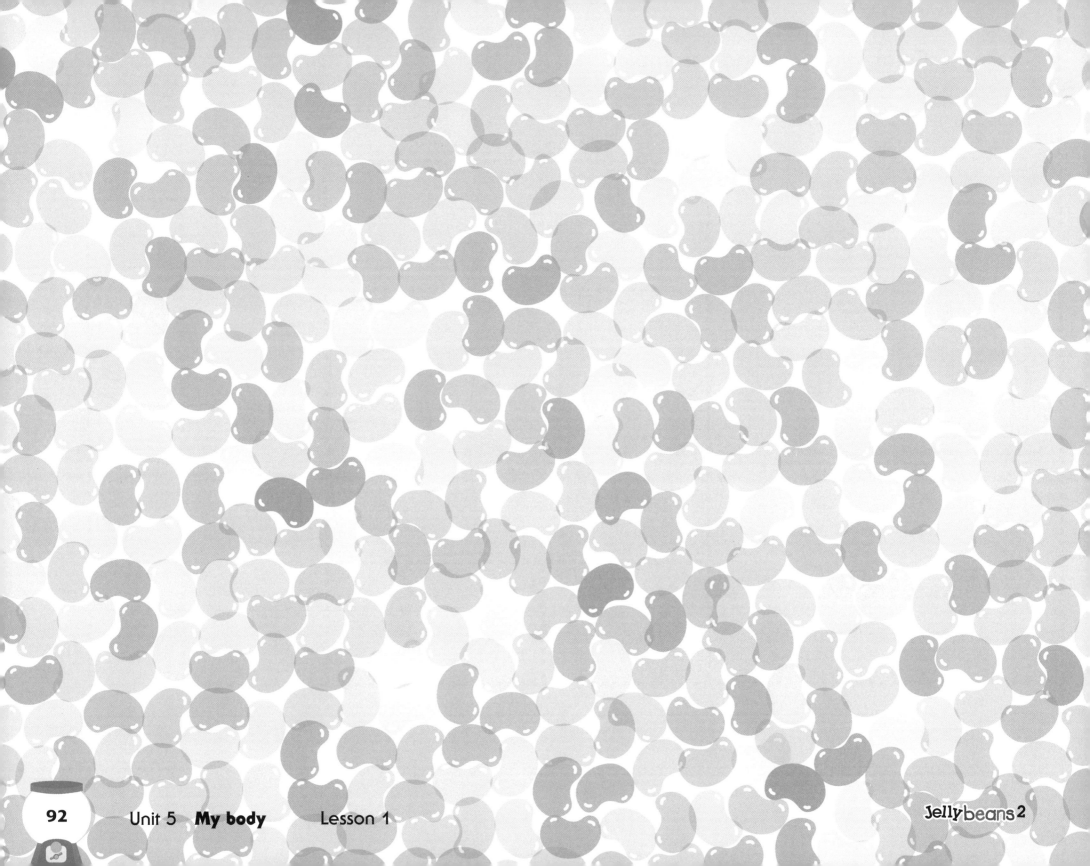

Jellybeans 2

Cut, glue and paint.

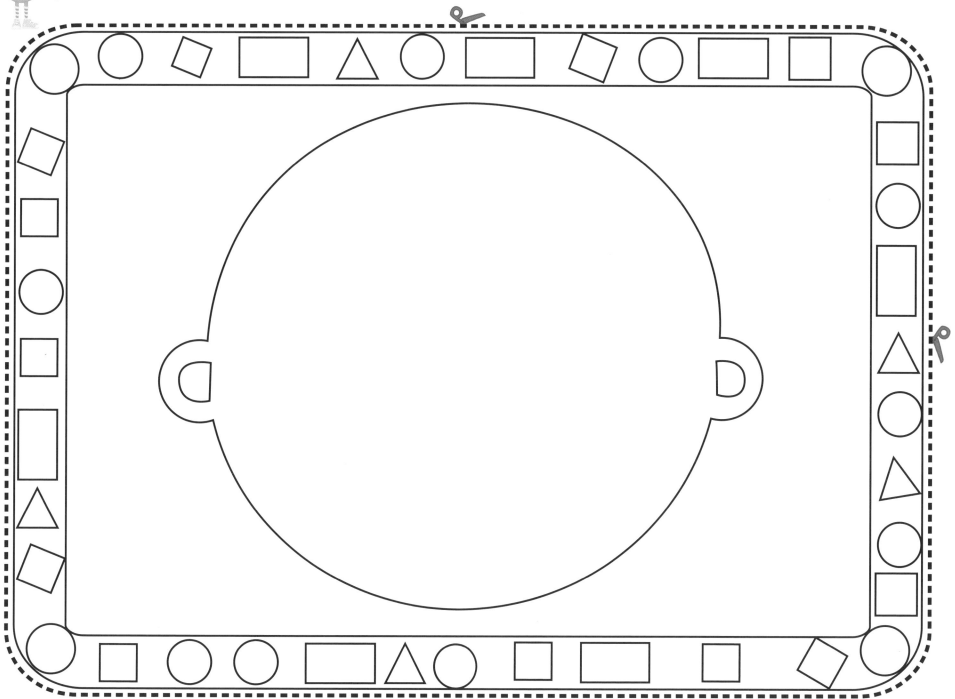

Color, cut and play *Concentration*.

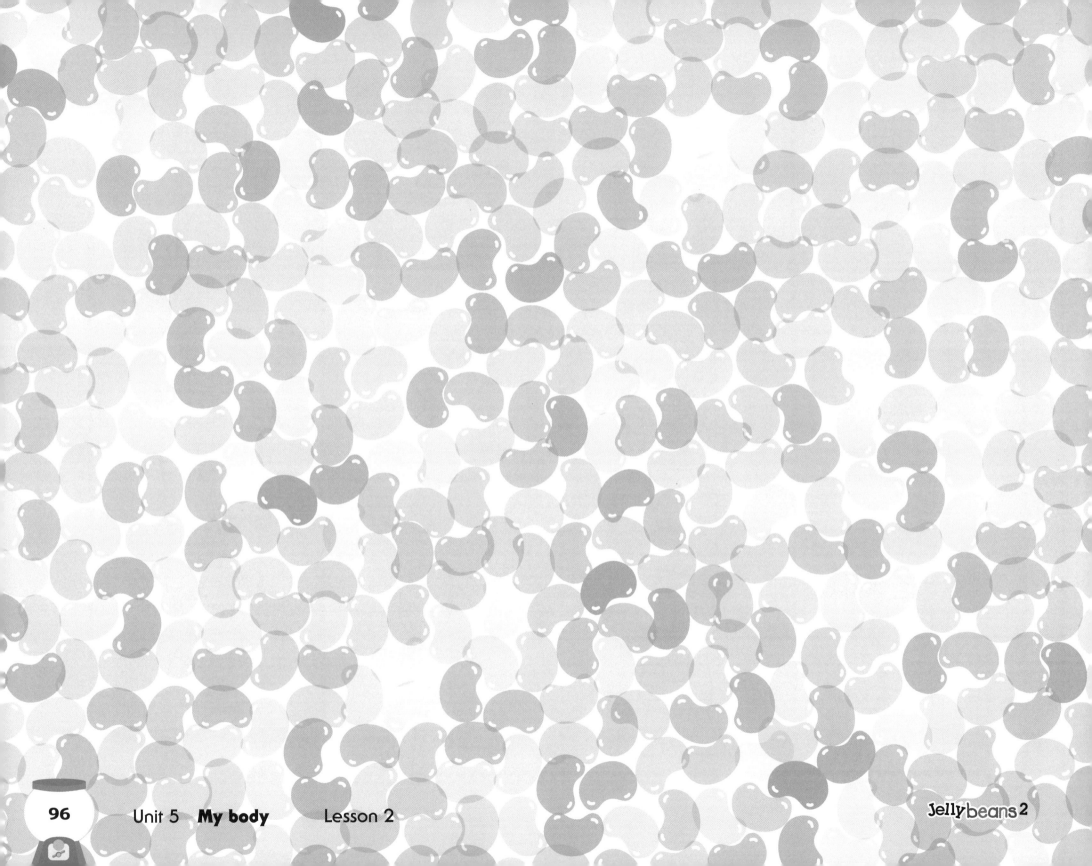

Jellybeans 2

Finger-paint and cut.

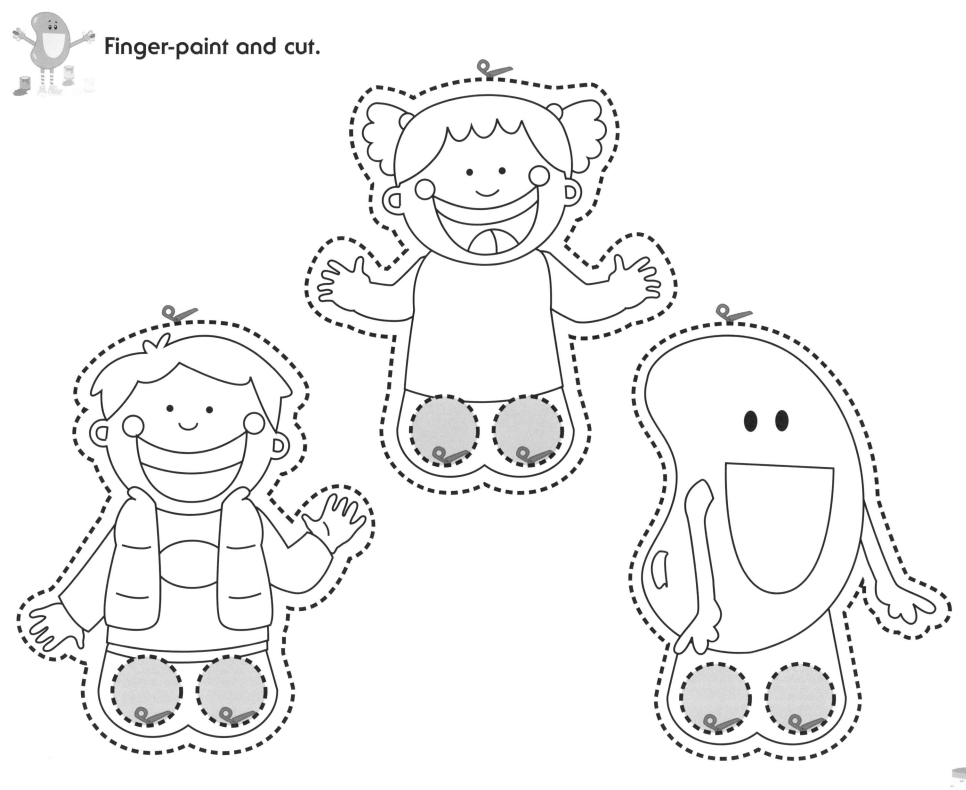

Jellybeans 2

Color, cut and assemble.

 Paint, glue and cut.

Unit 6 **Clothes and weather**   Lesson 1

Jellybeans2

Count, trace, color and paint.

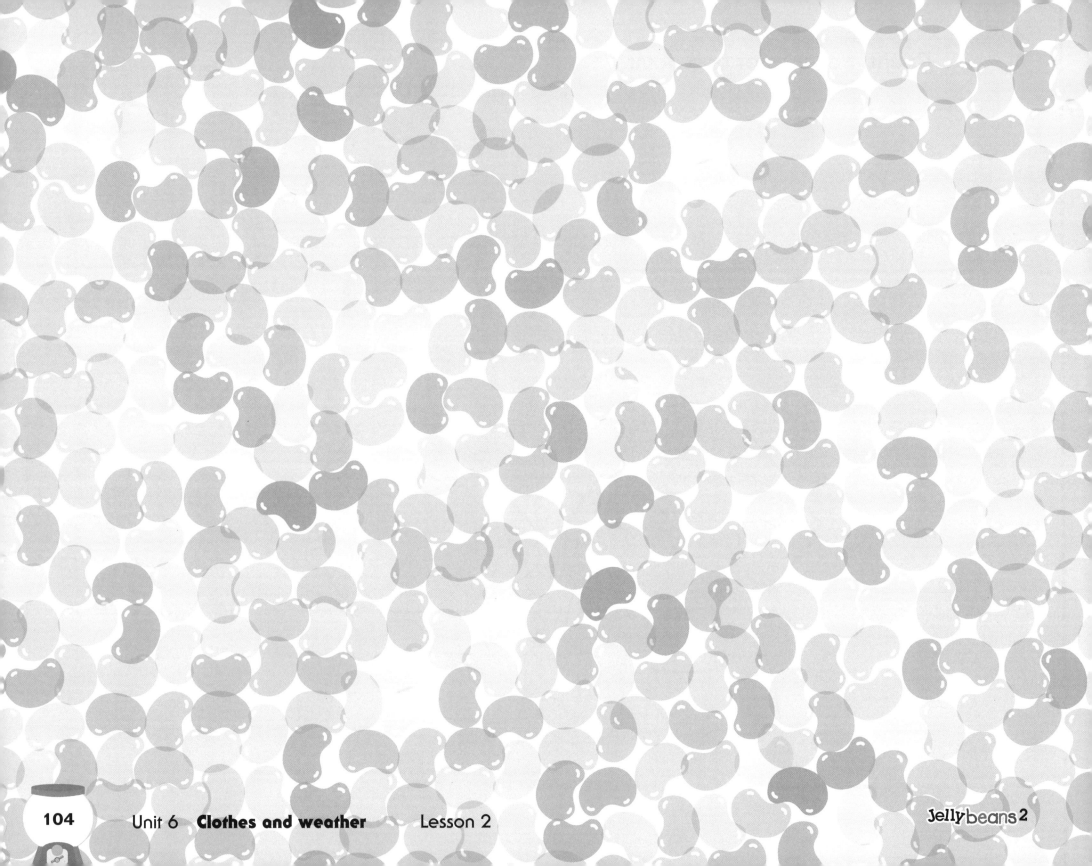

Color, cut, glue and assemble.

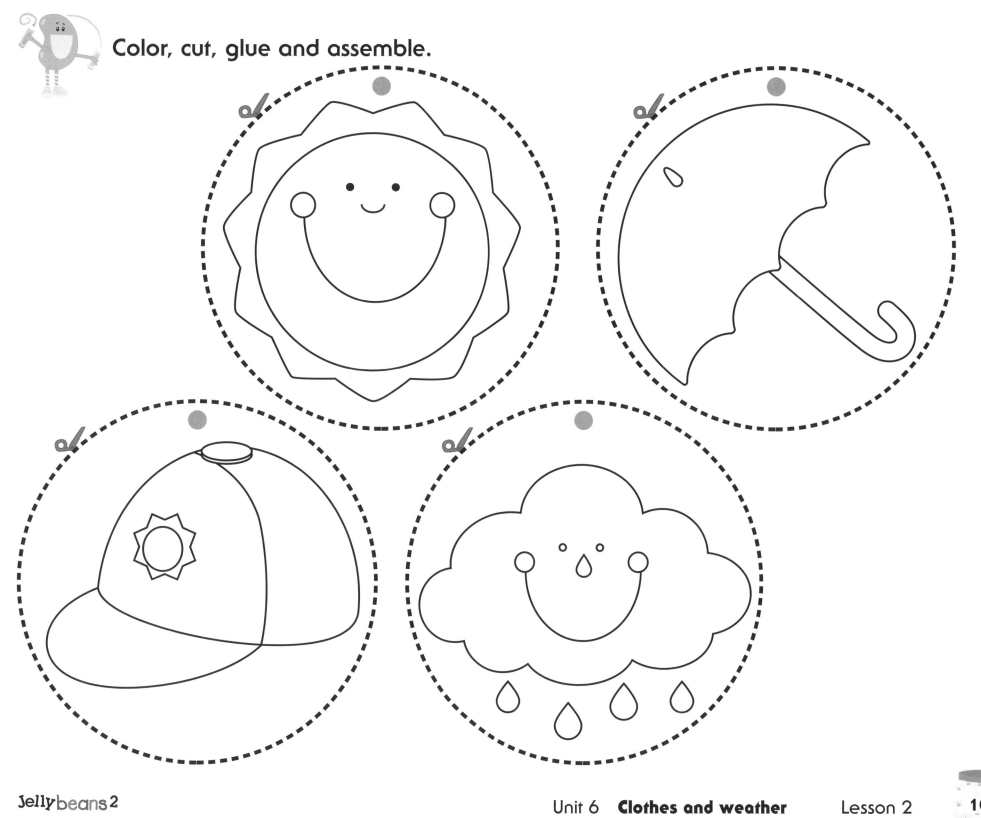

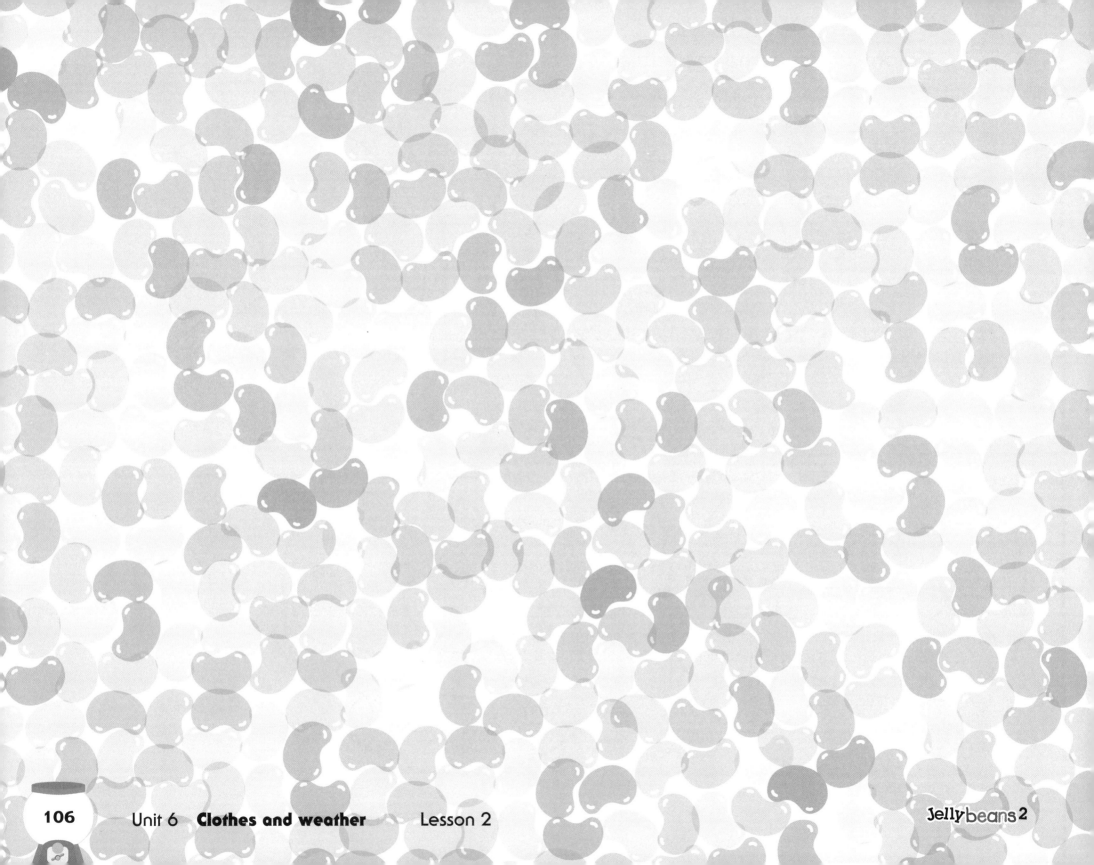

Jellybeans 2

Color, cut, fold and assemble.

Fold

Fold

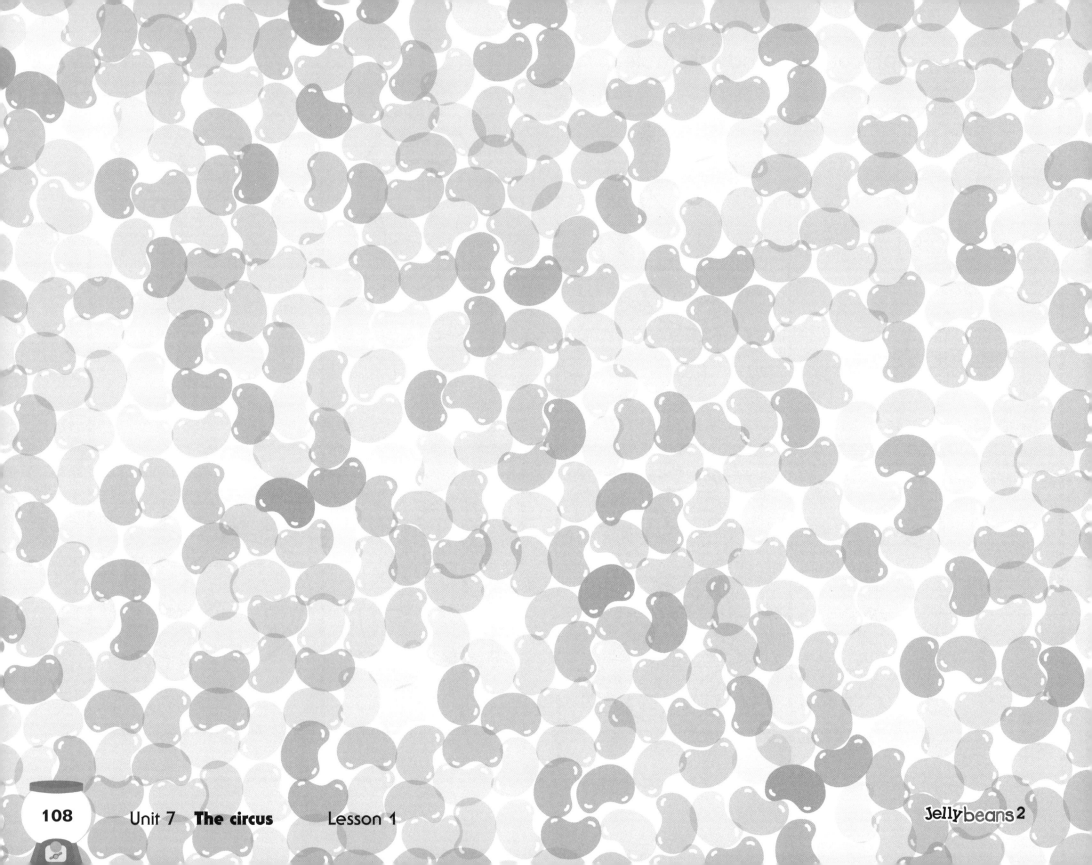

Paint, cut and assemble.

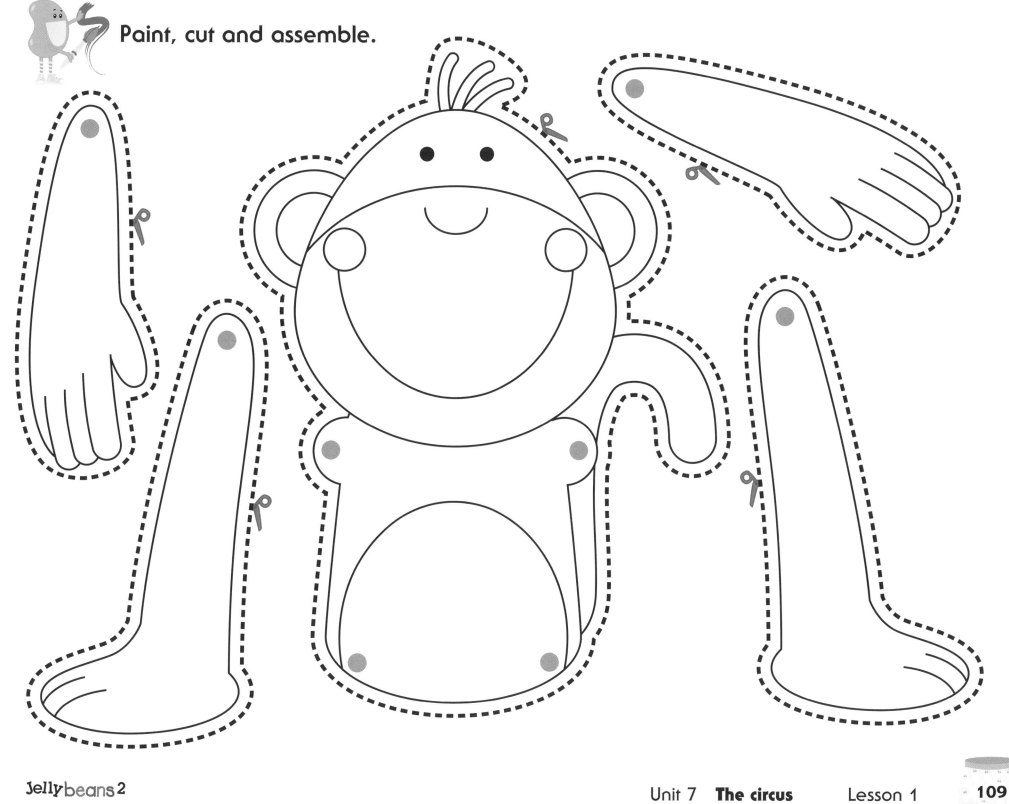

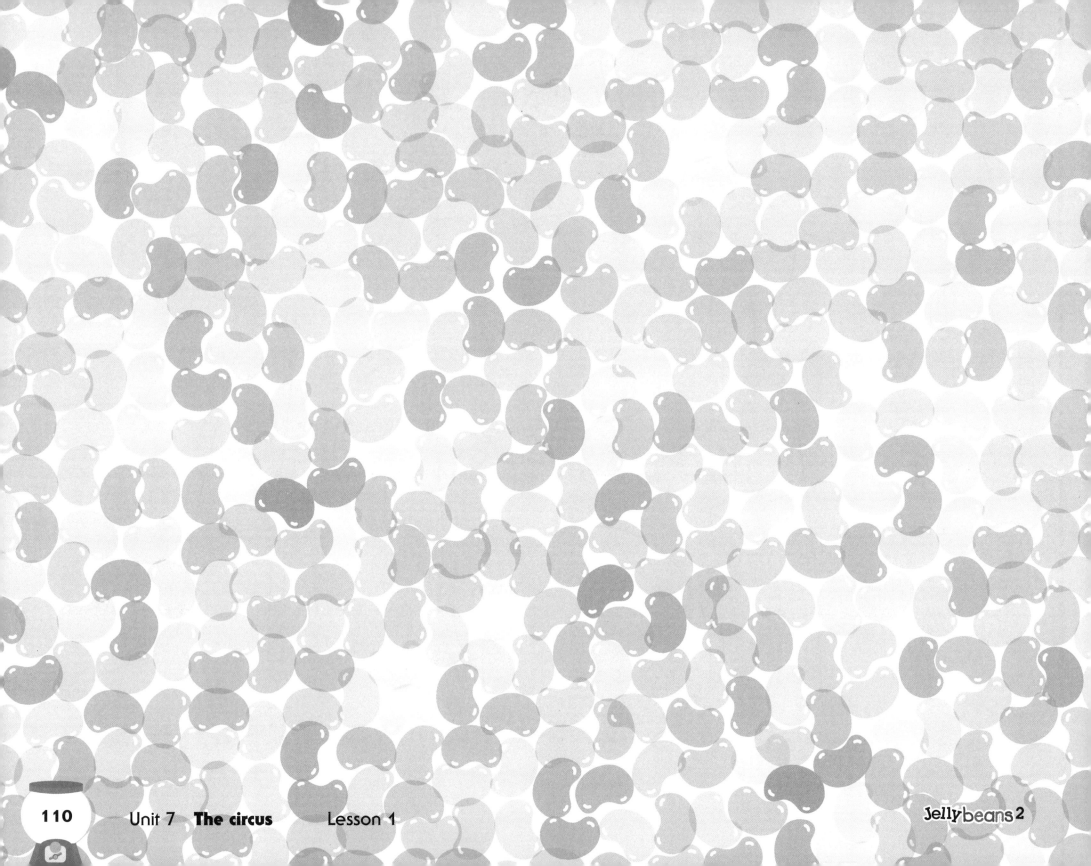

Jelly beans 2

Color, glue, cut and assemble.

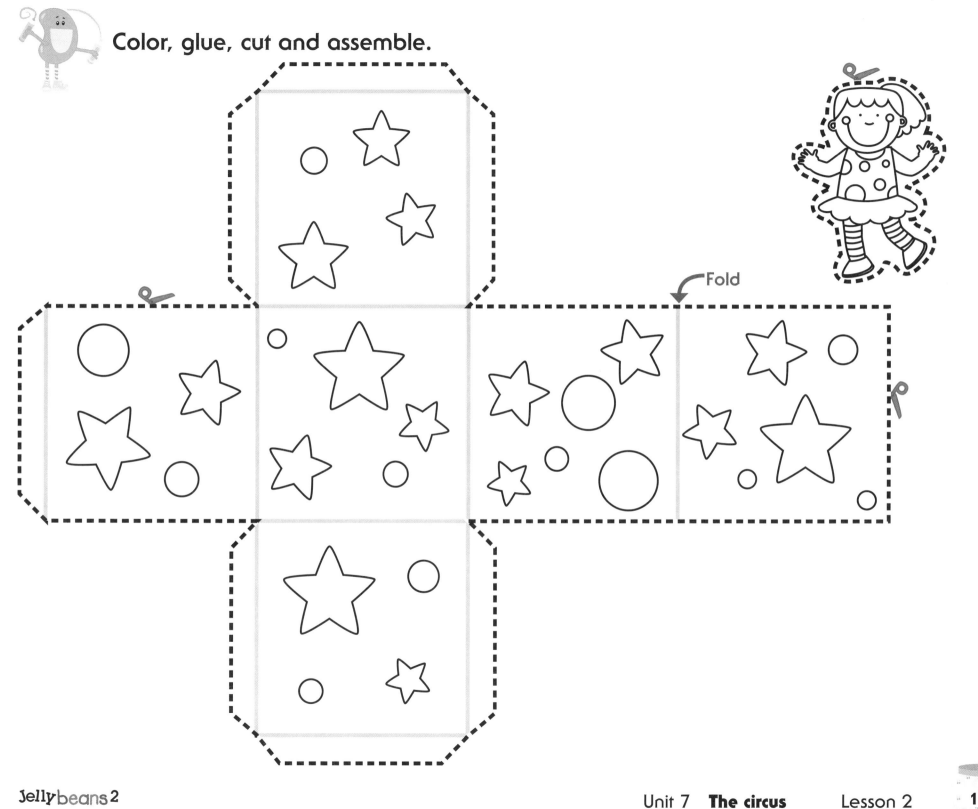

Fold

Color, cut and assemble.

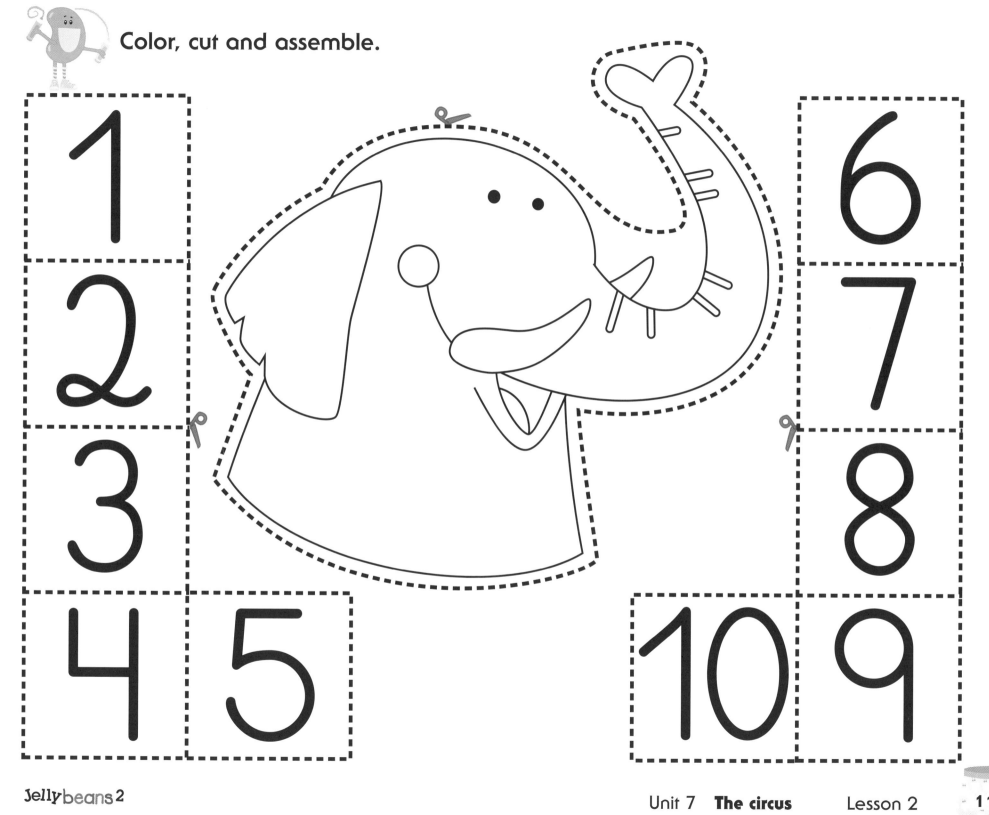

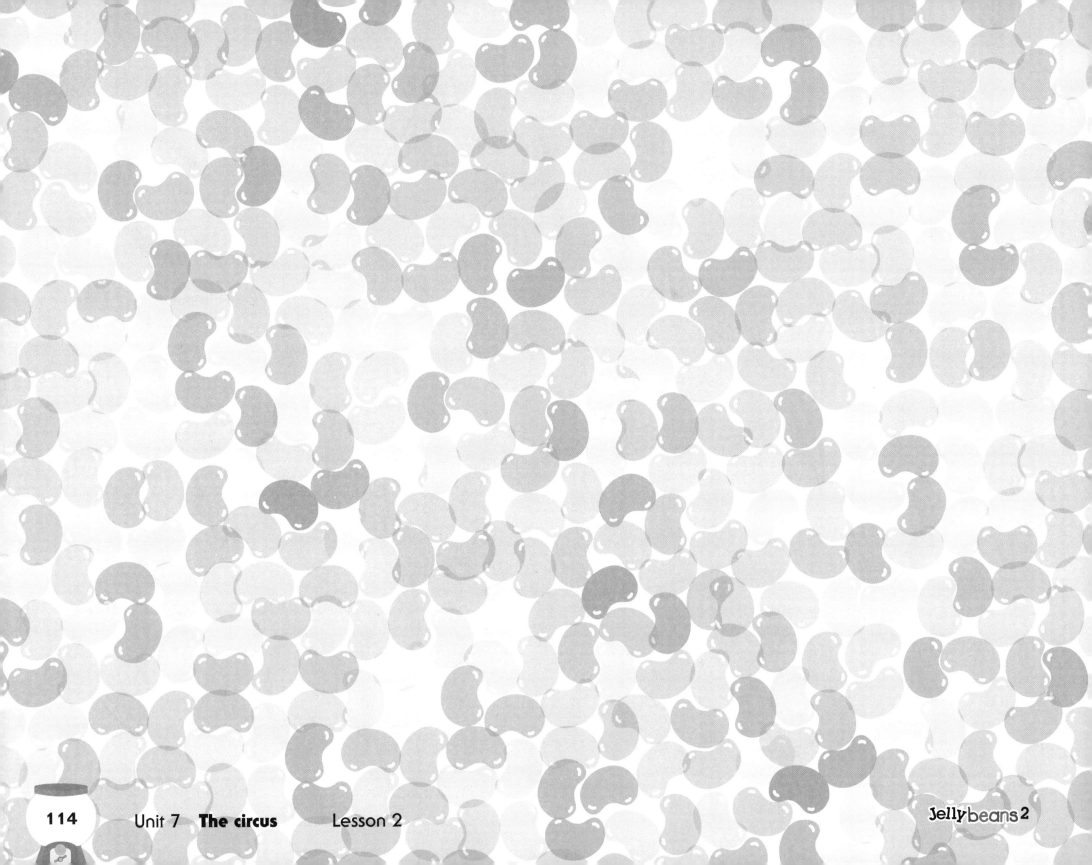

Color and cut.

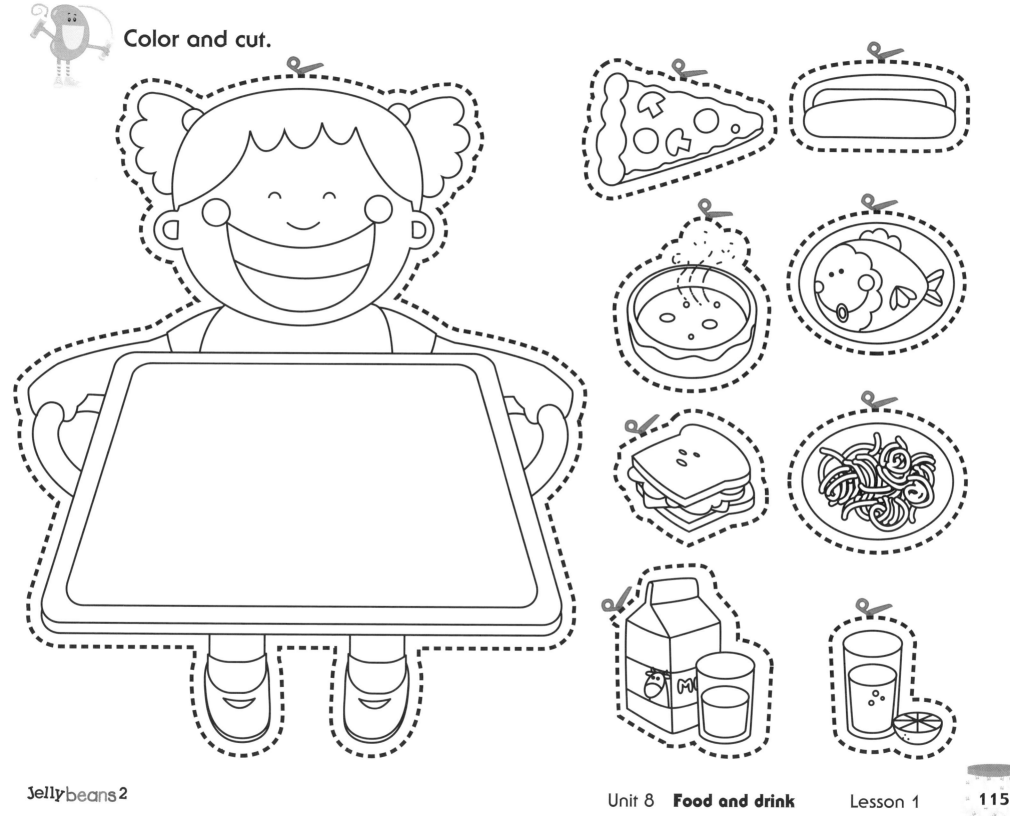

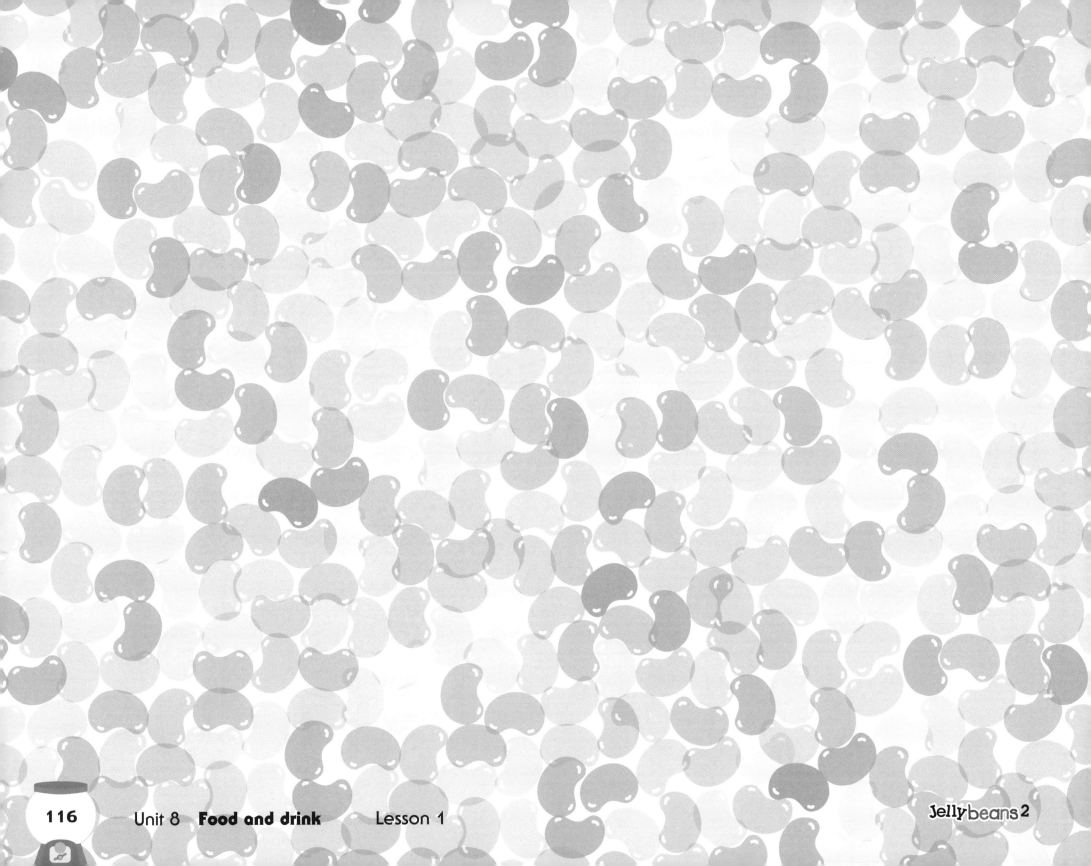

Unit 8 **Food and drink**   Lesson 1

Jellybeans 2

Color, paint, cut and assemble.

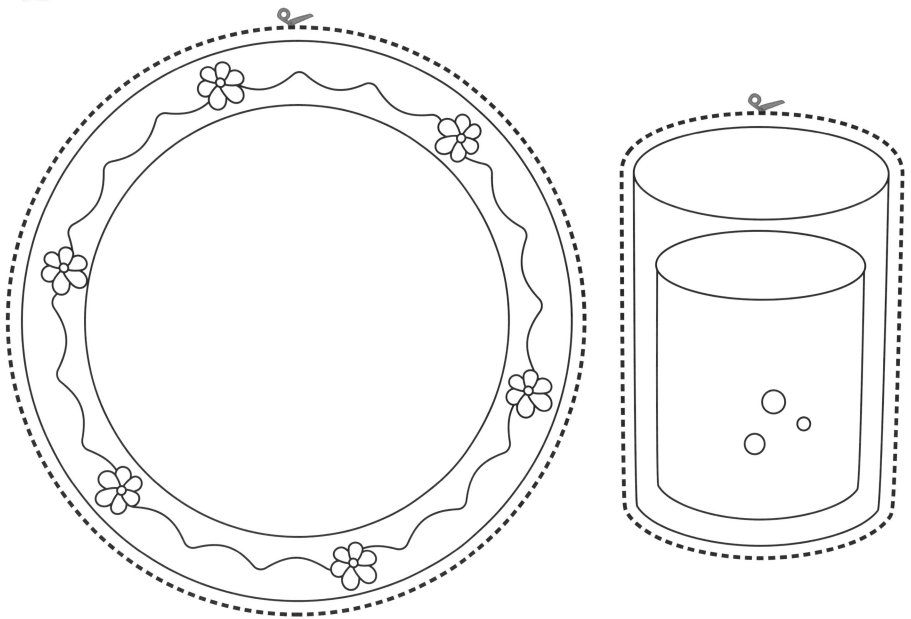

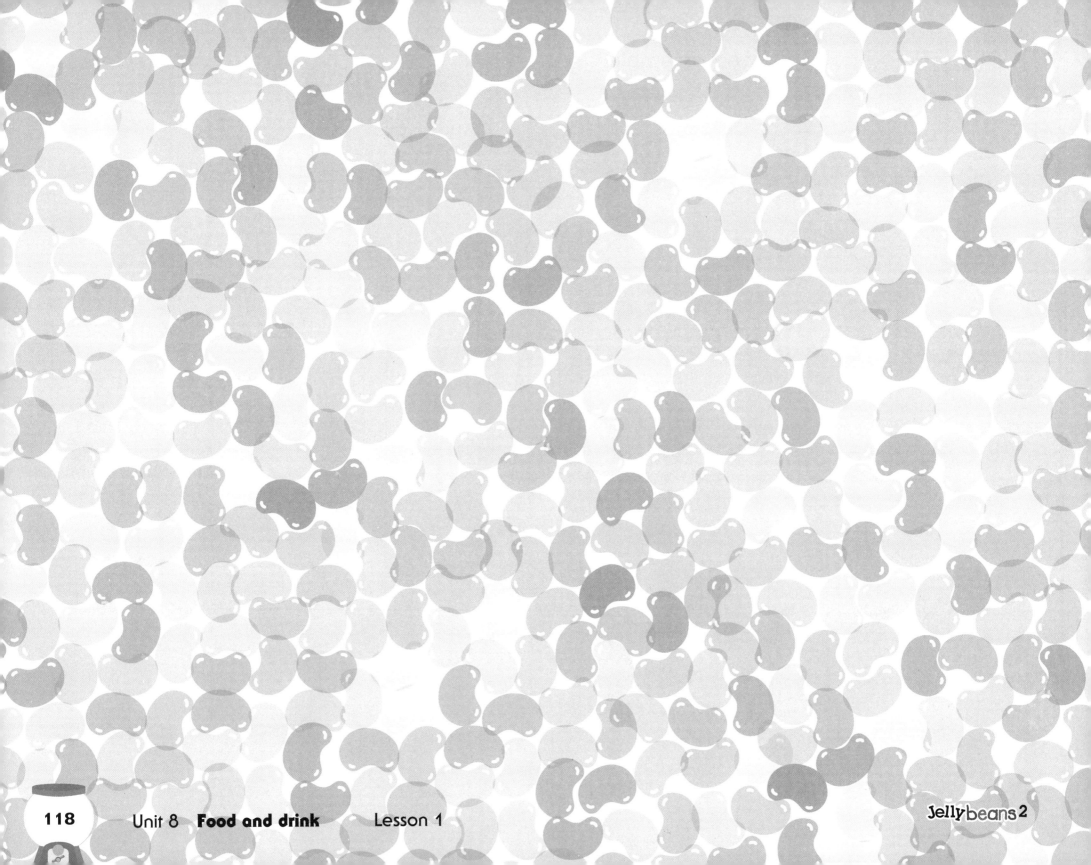

Cut, glue and color.

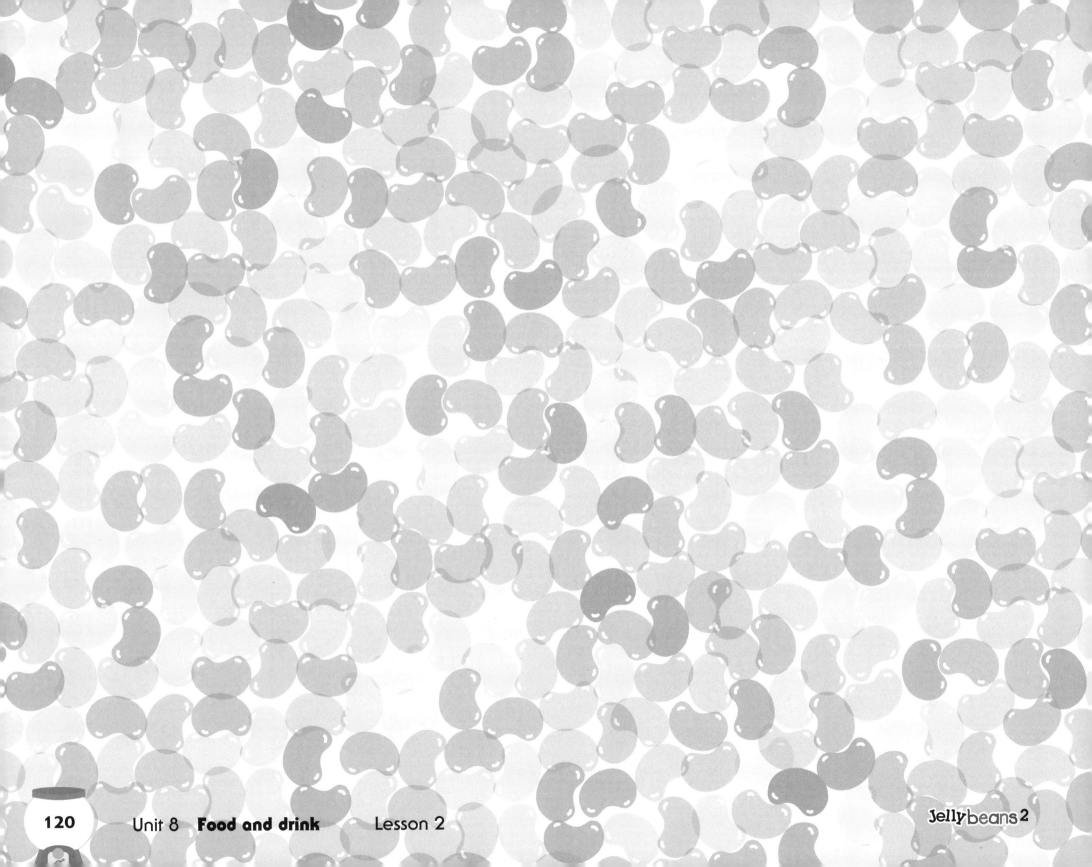

Jellybeans 2

Color, cut and assemble.

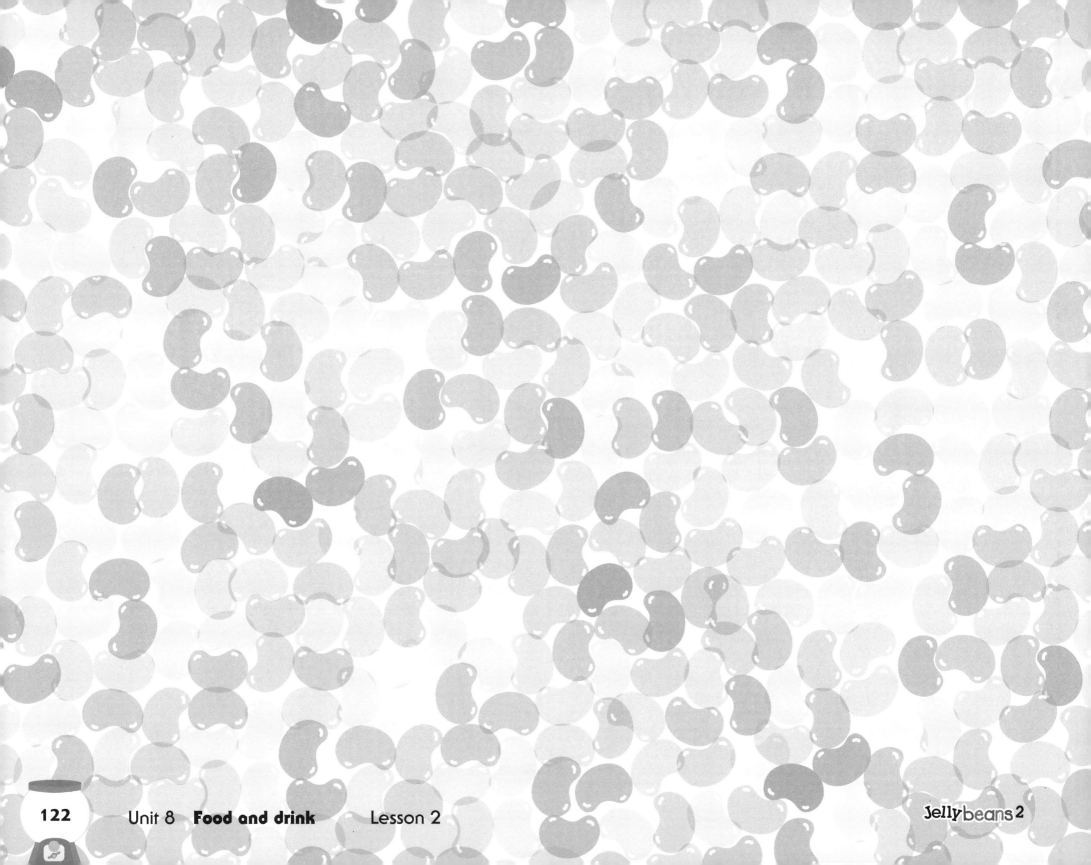

Jellybeans 2

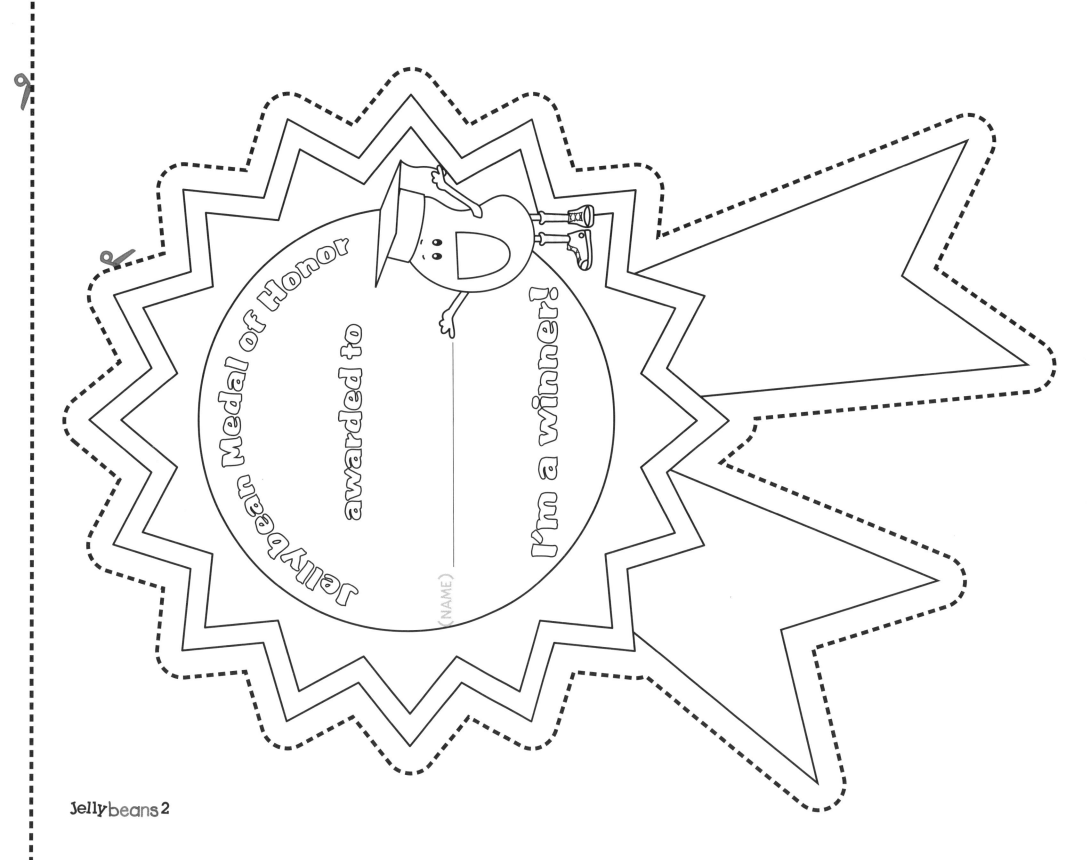

Jellybean Medal of Honor

awarded to

(NAME)

I'm a winner!

Jelly beans 2

jellybeans 2

Tracks

2 Hello, my friends	16 Left and right
3 Good-bye, my friends	17 Use your feet
4 You pick your pencil up	18 Walking, walking
5 Clean up, everybody	19 Put your finger on the clothes
6 Happy days cheer	20 It is sunny
7 Point to red	21 It is rainy
8 The shape song	22 Eensy weensy spider
9 Where is Father?	23 Funny clown
10 Where are they?	24 Circus parade
11 Old MacDonald	25 I'm going to the circus
12 Animal sounds	26 Do your best!
13 Five little ducks	27 Yummy, yum, yum
14 Body parts	28 This is the way I eat my breakfast
15 Hokey pokey	29 I eat pancakes

RICHMOND

58 St. Aldates
Oxford, OX1 1ST
England

Publisher: *Alicia Becker*
Executive Editors: *Alejandra Zapiain, Kimberley Silver*
Proofreader: *Lawrence Lipson*

Design Supervisor: *Marisela Pérez*
Design and Art Direction: *Marilú Jiménez*
Cover Design: *Marilú Jiménez*
Cover Illustration: *Raúl García*
DTP and Layout: *Claudia Rocha*
Technical Department: *Daniel Santillán, Edgar Colín,*
  José Luis Ávila, Salvador Pereira

Illustrations: *Claudia Navarro, Fabiola Graullera, Isabel Arnaud,*
  Javier Montiel, Lourdes Ponce, Marissa Arroyo, Teresa Martínez

First Edition: D.R. © Richmond Publishing, S.A. de C.V., 2008

This Edition: © Editora Moderna Ltda., 2011.
Editor: *Carla Montenegro*
Pedagogical Consultant: *Silvia Teles*
Copy Editor: *Sheila Winckler S. da Silva*
Proofreaders: *Camila Carmo da Silva, Katia Gouveia Vitale, Mariana*
  Mininel de Almeida, Vivian M. Viccino
Designer: *Gláucia Koller*
Layout: *Yara Campi*
Impressão e Acabamento: *Gráfica RONA*
      Lote: 768405
      Cod: 24070755

Dados Internacionais de Catalogação na Publicação (CIP)
(Câmara Brasileira do Livro, SP, Brasil)

Salvador, Rebecca Williams
  Jelly beans, 2 : student's book / Rebecca Williams &
Katy Smith. — São Paulo : Moderna, 2011.

  Suplementado pelo manual do professor

  1. Inglês (Educação infantil) I. Smith, Katy. II. Título.

11-04418   CDD-372.21

Índices para catálogo sistemático:
1. Inglês : Educação infantil   372.21

ISBN 978-85-16-07075-5 (LA)
ISBN 978-85-16-07076-2 (LP)

RICHMOND

EDITORA MODERNA LTDA.
Rua Padre Adelino, 758 – Belenzinho
São Paulo – SP – Brasil – CEP 03303-904
Central de atendimento ao usuário: 0800 771 8181
www.richmond.com.br
2023

Impresso no Brasil

Stickers

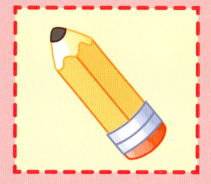

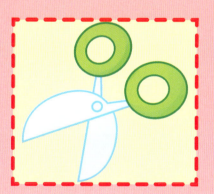

2 3

4 5